SATURDAY MORNING
MIND
CONTROL

PHIL PHILLIPS

OLIVER
NELSON

A Division of Thomas Nelson Publishers
Nashville

This book is dedicated to my friend, partner, and wife,
Cynthia, *and to our children,* **Taylor, Hayes,** *and* **Corbin,**
who bring us overwhelming joy each day.

And a very special thanks to our friends
James *and* **Noelle.** *We love and appreciate you.*

Copyright © 1991 by Phil Phillips

All rights reserved. Written permission must be secured from the publisher to use or reproduce any part of this book, except for brief quotations in critical reviews or articles.

Published in Nashville, Tennessee, by Oliver-Nelson Books, a division of Thomas Nelson, Inc., Publishers, and distributed in Canada by Lawson Falle, Ltd., Cambridge, Ontario.

Unless otherwise noted, the Bible version used in this publication is THE NEW KING JAMES VERSION. Copyright © 1979, 1980, 1982, Thomas Nelson, Inc., Publishers.

Printed in the United States of America.

ISBN 0-8407-9581-5

1 2 3 4 5 6 — 96 95 94 93 92 91

Contents

To schedule Phil Phillips for interviews and speaking engagements, write to:

Child Affects
P.O. Box 68
Rockwall, TX 75087
Or call: (214) 771-9839 FAX (214) 722-1721

Introduction

The Tale of
Young Child and The Box

Once upon a time there lived a little boy or girl named Young Child
—a child you know and love.

One day as Young Child was being rocked in his mother's arms,
he noticed a sound coming from the corner of the big room in which
mother and Young Child often sat together.

The sound was that of music. Big music. Fast music. Bigger and
faster music than that made by the little pillow in Young Child's
crib but, nonetheless, music. Young Child turned to see what made
this bigger, faster, more exciting sound.

And it was then that Young Child saw The Box.

What new thing is this? asked Young Child. It was the first time
Young Child had noticed The Box.

What bright colors it had and how they flashed! Little bits of color
moved every which way, lines and circles making all sorts of patterns. And all that music, too! Young Child was fascinated.

And behold, every now and then there were faces in The Box. To
be sure, they were flatter faces than those of mom and dad, but,
nonetheless, they were faces. They made the sounds that mom and
dad made. Well, sorta. And sometimes there were littler faces, like
little people, sorta. And what was that? Why, laughter! Young Child

knew about laughter. Mom and dad had been trying to make Young Child laugh ever since Young Child was born. Young Child was good at laughing.

Young Child looked again the next time mother carried him into the big room. Sure enough, The Box was still there. And the next day, too. And the next, and the next, and the next. *The Box must live here,* thought Young Child.

Sometimes The Box looked dull and gray. No people, no colors, no music, no laughter. What a mystery! But those times weren't very often or for very long. Most of the time, The Box was there in all its glory, sending forth its music, its talking, its laughter, and its bright colors and flat faces.

One day Young Child tried to talk to The Box. But it wouldn't listen. It just went right on talking, and laughing, and playing its music. *What The Box is saying must be more important than what I am saying,* thought Young Child. And so Young Child listened.

One day Young Child asked, "What do you mean, Box? I don't understand you." But The Box wouldn't explain itself. It just went right on talking, and laughing, and playing its music. The people didn't even stop moving. *What The Box is telling must be more important than what I am asking,* thought Young Child. So Young Child began to watch The Box more closely. Surely it must mean something. Surely it must have some answers.

Young Child watched, and watched, and watched.

By the time Young Child had turned into Young Adult, Young Child had watched 22,000 hours of what The Box said and showed. In fact, Young Child had watched The Box more than he had gone to school (only 11,000 hours) or played with dad (only 4,000 hours). In fact, Young Child had watched The Box more than he had done anything else in his life except sleep.

Young Adult no longer asked what The Box meant. It wasn't that Young Adult had the answer. The question just didn't seem to matter any more.

One of the most amazing facts of the last fifty years is that The Box—the television set and all its programming—has become such a familiar and endlessly available entity in our lives.

For the most part, the television day begins between six and seven

A.M., and ends at one or two A.M. In all, more than 184 million TV sets are in operation in the United States, and more than half of them are turned on at this very moment. The facts surrounding TV usage are staggering.

- Approximately 88.6 million U.S. homes (98 percent) now have at least one TV set, and 60 percent of U.S. homes have two or more TV sets. Fifty-three percent of American homes have videocassette recorders.

- A. C. Nielsen Company data show that children ages two to five watch an average of 28 hours a week of television, and children between the ages of six and eleven watch an average of 23.5 hours a week. All ages considered, the average American child will watch 27.3 hours of TV this week.

- Preschoolers are spending more time watching TV than it will take them in the future to earn a college degree. By the time the American child has completed high school, he will have watched 22,000 hours of TV—11,000 hours more than he will have spent in classrooms.

- Stated another way, the average American child spends as much as one-third of his day in passive contemplation of a TV screen. By the time a child of today reaches the age of seventy, he will have spent about seven years watching TV—a full one-tenth of his life, including sleeping hours!

Approximately 250,000 TV sets are made in the United States every day. And approximately 250,000 children are born in America every day. Sadly, TV is often a more demanding presence in a home than a crying infant is.

In many cases, TV has not only joined the family, it has become the family! Children frequently get to know the shows and stars of network programs as well as or better than their cousins, aunts and uncles, grandparents, and godparents.

Television today is considered a *personal necessity,* even as stated by law. New York Governor Hugh Carey signed a bill on July 28, 1976, exempting a TV set from being appropriated to satisfy money judgment. The Box joined the "utensils necessary for the judgment debtor and family" along with wearing apparel, household furniture, tableware, pots and pans, and so forth.

As Joan Anderson Wilkins wrote in *Breaking the TV Habit:*

> In the early days of television, the medium was a dessert, something families shared after dinner, after daily chores, after talk time, and after homework. But what started out as dessert in the 1950's has now become the whole meal from soup to nuts.

Television has become the dictator of family routines in many homes, with family members often adjusting themselves to its programming schedules. One research study by Clara T. Appell reported that 60 percent of the families she surveyed had changed their sleep patterns and 55 percent had changed their eating schedules to accommodate television.

And sadly, some 78 percent of the population Dr. Appell studied reported that it frequently used TV as a baby-sitter.

Sadly, another study reports that only about a third of all parents even *attempt* to control the amount and content of the TV their children watch.

Sadly, most American parents consider TV to be one of their children's foremost playmates and, in some cases, their only playmate.

Why *sadly?* Because most of these parents probably never stop to ask themselves a critical question: *What kind of a playmate is TV for a child?*

PART
1

Playmate or Teacher?

Chapter One

What Kind of a Playmate Is TV?

There was a child went forth every day and the first object he looked upon and received with wonder or pity or love or dread, that object he became. And that object became part of him for the day or a certain part of the day . . . or for many years or stretching cycles of years.

These became part of that child who went forth every day and who now goes and will always go forth every day. And these become of him or her that peruses them now.

—Walt Whitman
LEAVES OF GRASS

Play is what your child does with his days. By the time the average American child is seven years old, he will have logged 15,000 hours in playtime. All his classroom time from kindergarten through a baccalaureate degree will also amount to 15,000 hours.

Why Play?

In many ways, play is a child's true primary education. But what does a child learn through play? Perhaps the more important question is, What is play to a child?

Play is fun; it represents something positive and pleasurable to a child. True play has no extrinsic goals. Its motivations are purely intrinsic. Play happens because the child (or adult, even) chooses to play. Play is spontaneous and voluntary.

Work and play are not true opposites. Work is a mathematically measurable quantity of effort or exertion of power. Play, on the other hand, is measured strictly in subjective terms or in terms of emotional quality.

Watch a three-year-old at play and you are likely to find a child totally absorbed in the work of building with blocks, extremely frustrated when an older brother knocks them over, sad when part of the building falls down. You may conclude that nothing about that play activity is fun, but to the child, fun is involved. Play is always desirable and rewarding at the emotional level.

Play is active. That characteristic is vital to a child's physical development because in early childhood the large muscle groups are developed. This happens primarily through gross motor play by his climbing on frames, riding bicycles, and learning mastery over large mobile objects and tools.

Fine muscle and motor coordination, as well as manipulative skills and eye-hand coordination, also begin to develop through the handling of smaller items, such as stacking building blocks or turning the pages of a book. These skills are critical to a child's later development, and they begin to be acquired about the age of two.

At the age of three, the child becomes more social in nature, seeking out others with whom to play. The child is growing rapidly during this time, and activities that provide strength and dexterity are important. This is generally the age of rough-and-tumble play, as a child learns how to use the body and begins to explore ways of relating to others beyond immediate family members.

The ages of four and five are important for developing large muscles and for coping with growth spurts by readjusting coordination.

Throughout this preschool period, the child learns best by interacting with people and with concrete objects. In this way, through play, a child learns about shapes, sizes, weight, and forms—information and skills critical to all other areas of learning in the future. A child learns through play how to grasp and manipulate objects of different shapes. He develops finger dexterity. He learns the concepts of space and time. He begins to understand how his body moves through space and at what speeds. He learns about gravity.

The child learns how things can be divided and put back together into wholes; how pieces of things fit together; and the differences among various angles. She learns the way things connect, whether sticks, dots, or the cars on a train are involved. In all of this exploration, the child is learning certain basic mathematical relationships that adults take for granted.

Throughout, play is always a form of experimental inquiry. If one experiment doesn't work, the child will try another way, another method, another means.

In play, a child learns not to give up at the first sign of failure;

play builds persistence. The child gains the skills of concentration that he will need later for problem solving.

Through play, a child tests her hypotheses of the world. And in having control over this testing process, a child gains confidence.

Play gives a child a sense of autonomy and builds self-esteem. Through play, he says, "I am a distinct individual and I can control this toy and I can determine the outcome of this device, even if only in my fantasy."

Play is also the primary way a child learns how to relate to others. Children learn the art of play by imitating others, usually their parents, who first play with them to make them laugh. Children learn how to play with toys when parents show them how to use toys. They catch on quickly, but they must first see how to play.

To this end, a child's play can be greatly enhanced by the presence of and periodic interaction with an adult. A parent can help a child focus attention by pointing to an object, by moving an object, by showing the child how something operates, by asking questions, by naming objects, and by suggesting pretend play to prime the pump of a child's own imagination.

Educators often refer to two main types of play: dramatic and sociodramatic play.

In dramatic play a child mimics adult actions. The child may play fire engine driver, for example. The child imagines circumstances, objects, and verbal communication. The child often is persistent in his scenario until the action has been satisfactorily completed—in our example, until the fire has been put out!

Sociodramatic play includes at least two players. The verbal interaction from child to child is real, and characters are possible in role-playing. Each child brings elements of imagination to the construction of the plot, the pretend environment, and the circumstances encountered. Such play allows the child to display his own physical abilities, and it creates a social awareness about what is satisfying both at the child level and, through rewards, at the adult level.

Sociodramatic play encourages the preschooler to develop concepts of different social roles and to associate relevant behaviors with those roles. A child is likely to choose a dominant role (doctor) over a passive one (patient), an active role (ballplayer) over an inactive one (coach).

Dramatic play and sociodramatic play are especially important for children ages seven to twelve. Nearly all play during those ages is interpersonal. Children learn through play to share grief, challenges, affection, and secrets with one another. They develop concepts of loyalty; they join the club, the team, or the secret group. If a child misses out on this stage, he often has great difficulty forming relationships with his peers when he hits the teen years.

Children learn to recognize their own feelings through play. They begin to understand that they have a variety of feelings that relate somehow to other people. And they learn how to resolve those feelings.

For example, a child may experience sadness or rejection when he isn't included in a game. She may be frustrated when she can't hit the softball. He may get angry when someone doesn't play fair. Often these feelings are resolved on the playground without adult intervention. At other times, adults need to help a child understand his or her feelings and suggest appropriate behaviors.

Children often use play to work through and master complex psychological difficulties, of both the past and the present. Play is a critical part of many forms of therapy in child psychology and child psychiatry.

A child uses play to resolve his own past behaviors. We often see a child spank a doll for something the child himself has done.

A child may use play to resolve something unknown or feared in the present. A toddler might resort to being a baby or treating her doll like a baby as she hears her mother talk about the imminent arrival of a brother or sister. The child is already hearing so much about this other person that she's experiencing anxiety over him; if being a new baby is all that great, she wants to try it out for herself!

Play is also the prime time when a child tries out language for himself. Very early in their development, children learn that words can be a form of pleasure, fun, and jokes.

Children from six to twelve find word games rewarding. The child is then learning to read, her basic syntactic development is virtually complete, and she is acquiring vocabulary. He enjoys word jokes, puns, riddles, tongue twisters, and other forms of wordplay. The child also finds new play in her ability to talk to others and to make up stories that include full-blown dialogue.

Even during the preschool years, however, play increases a child's opportunities for communication; thus it helps develop communication skills.

Play is a time for a child to test fantasy against reality. Children are involved in fantasy play from about the age of three. Many of their perceptions up to the age of eight or nine are entirely fantasy. Experiences are woven and rewoven with new circumstances, visualizations, and dialogues.

Fantasy play helps a child explore the limits of reality. Imaginings are those moments when a child can ask himself, What if? A child can move from one part of the world to another, from the present to the future, and back into the past. Through imaginings, a child tries out conflicting views and alternative outcomes. He learns that reality limits many kinds of behavior. Without flights of fantasy, he can't truly get to know his interests or make responsible choices in adulthood.

Play is a time for making choices. True creative play occurs when the child begins to play with something and doesn't have a preconceived idea about what will happen.

For example, give a child some clay or some other malleable material and watch what happens. She'll begin to form it into shapes and soon combine it by colors and shapes. Sometimes she'll get shells, feathers, seeds, stones, or other objects to combine with the goo. She may not have started out to make a particular item, but through the process of play, she ends up with an original artifact. A similar thing happens with a set of paints, an easel, and blank pieces of paper.

Through creative play, a child's concept of beauty begins to be formed. A child begins to develop his or her own taste. Children see shapes and colors and feel textures that they like or dislike. It's not uncommon to see a three-year-old pick particular blooms from a patch of flowers. They were the ones the child thought were the prettiest or most interesting.

In summary, children learn sensory and motor skills from play. They also develop intellectual and communication skills, gain emotional awareness, and learn social behavior through play. The best kind of play stimulates a child's mental abilities and promotes curiosity.

Education researchers have found that children's mental abilities are stimulated when they are allowed to explore freely their surroundings and have a variety of interesting materials around them. Other researchers have found that children who play outdoors are less aggressive, more mature, and more cooperative. Their games tend to be longer and more complex than those who play only indoors (Minuchin and Shapiro 1983). Children who play indoors without television develop creative and experimental abilities, and they also often have better small-motor skills.

Still other educators have found that when materials around a child are not varied, the child plays less with the items that are available than a child who has a variety of materials from which to choose. The children without variety tend to do a lot more watching, waiting, or idle cruising (Clarke-Stewart 1982).

Children need stimulation. They need freedom to explore and space in which to move.

Can TV Be a Playmate?

How does all this relate to TV as a playmate? Television does absolutely nothing to help a child grow in any of the play abilities described above.

Television does not help a child develop gross motor and fine motor skills, improve dexterity, or develop spatial or manipulative skills with concrete objects.

A television set doesn't combine with anything. It doesn't give a true picture of size. The characters are limited to the size of a TV screen—in many cases, not larger than twenty inches tall!

Television does not help a child make up sentences, communicate with other people, or develop spontaneous word games.

Television does not provide a child a buddy with whom to romp on the floor or with whom the child might engage in sociodramatic skills.

Television does nothing to help a child explore the full gamut of feelings or learn how to resolve feelings through play. Most programs, with the possible exceptions of "Mister Rogers" and "Pee-Wee Herman," do little to help a child recognize and define feelings.

Some programs exhibit feelings. "Care Bears" is all about feelings. Grumpy Bear, Love-a-lot Bear, and Funshine Bear all exude feelings. Their message to a child is that it's okay to have feelings, and that not everybody feels the same way all the time. That isn't the same, however, as helping a child explore his or her own feelings to discover societally appropriate ways of expressing them.

Television does not enhance a child's creativity or his ability to imagine or create fantasy. Television portrays someone else's imaginings and robs the child of supplying his own.

Television does not lead a child to ask the What if? question. It says to the child, "This is what," and provides a prescription for reality, even though television does not portray the real world around the child. Adults must realize that fantasy is not a false reality. It's a setting aside of true reality. A good fantasy uses reality as a springboard and returns to it.

Television does not provide the variety, the freedom to move, or the problem-solving settings of outdoor or nontelevision indoor play.

Finally, television does not provide accurate information by which a child might develop societal behavior. Children need information about people, things, events, relationships, and symbols, accurate information about the way society works. It's a common practice on TV for someone to enter another person's house unannounced, to comment about the ring in a friend's toilet bowl, or to choose to eat at a friend's house without being invited. Adults may be able to overlook such behavior as exaggerated and abnormal. The child, however, sees such behavior as real. No check-and-balance system for interaction exists to lead a child to conclude that this type of behavior is not socially acceptable.

The sad news is that a child loses valuable experimental, active, social, and communicative playtime during every hour spent in front of The Box. Furthermore, there's no replacement for developmental time once it's lost.

Most psychologists believe that 80 percent of a child's character and personality has been developed by the time she is five years old. Others have reported that we learn 80 percent of all that we will ever learn during the first five years of life, including vocabulary, knowledge of the everyday world, and so forth.

With the time of childhood so critical on so many learning and developmental fronts, an hour spent making mud pies is always better than an hour spent watching television.

As far back as 1925 Arnold Gesell wrote this about child development:

> The brain grows at a tremendous rate during the preschool age, reaching its mature bulk before the age of six, and the mind develops at a corresponding velocity. The infant learns to see, hear, handle, walk, comprehend, and talk. He acquires an uncountable number of habits fundamental to the complex art of living. Never again will his mind, his character, his spirit advance as rapidly as in the formative preschool period of growth. Never again will we have an equal chance to lay the foundations for mental health. (28)

So What's a Parent to Do?

Watch your child at play without interrupting or commenting. Learn more about what play means to your child.

Sit down and play with your child and his toys. See what you can make with the blocks or dress a doll. Be a playmate. Don't teach or explain.

Remember that a parent can actually increase the level of a child's imaginative play by playing with the child—by introducing new ideas; by making suggestions about environment, objects, and circumstances; and by role-playing a character.

Encourage your child to play apart from television. Recognize that TV is not a suitable playmate. Turn off The Box and bring out the toys, or suggest that your child go outside to play.

Finally, be aware that television is not entertainment to a child. It is a teacher. And oh, the lessons it teaches.

Chapter Two

How TV Teaches Your Child

For me, TV is very educational, when it's on. I go into the other room and read a book.

—Comedian Groucho Marx

All television is educational television.

—Former Federal
Communications Commissioner
Nicholas Johnson

In the movie *Short Circuit,* a robot takes on human characteristics, and the first trait he displays is an insatiable desire for information. "Input, input," he demands of his human hostess. "I-n-p-u-t!"

Newborn children also display that trait among their first: children are born eager to learn. To understand how TV teaches, we must first understand something about how children learn.

How Do Children Learn?

A child learns from whatever gets his attention. A baby responds to noise contrasts: loud noises, strange noises, and sudden bursts of noise from silence.

He responds to visual objects that are unusual. Children as young as two-and-a-half months respond to motion and color. In a 1971 study with infants in an institution, Brossard and Decarie found that infants who were exposed to decorative mobiles and distinctive sounds didn't show the intellectual decline often found in institutionalized babies. The mobiles triggered the child's ability to attend to something outside himself.

Variety is critical to babies' development. One study involved five-month-old infants from a range of socioeconomic groups. The researchers found that the babies' later scores on tests of intelligence, problem-solving ability, object permanence, and exploration were directly related to the variety of objects available to them for stimulation (Yarrow, Rubenstein, and Pederson 1975).

A young child learns from what is concrete and especially from what he can feel in a tactile way. The tactile sense is the most important one to an infant. He wants to feel an object with his fingers and also to see how that object feels inside his mouth!

The child learns the difference between hard and soft, small and large, light and heavy. He learns about textures and spatial relationships. He learns which object causes pain (the hot stove) and which gives sensations of pleasure (his favorite blanket). He learns that an object can move on its own (the family cat) and that another can respond in an unusual way (the jack-in-the-box).

Feeling in a tactile way is the one method of learning that is most closely linked with the concept of doing. Over the years, educators have concluded that persons commit to memory and put into action about 10 percent of what they hear, 50 percent of what they see, and 90 percent of what they do.

What about TV?

What happens when a child is plopped down in front of a TV set? It moves. It has color and unusual sounds. It captures attention. But it can't be perceived by all of the child's senses, and most important, it can't be held. It has no feeling. As a result, what it portrays has no sensory meaning attached to it for the child.

Television doesn't really cause pain. It may cause eyestrain but rarely does it hurt to watch someone murdered on TV.

To hold a young child's attention, cartoons must be more interesting than the prevailing reality around him. Cartoons do this through a great deal of rapid motion, which has been shown to command attention in infants as young as four months. Cartoons also do this by emphasizing the unusual, the bizarre, and the unexpected.

Cartoons, while using a medium of reality, actually present few instances within the field of reality of a young child. More than any other time, Saturday morning is a time of illusion.

The problem is that young children don't know they are experiencing illusion. They believe what they see. They believe that somewhere out there, beyond their personal worlds, the world portrayed on Saturday mornings also exists.

In our questioning of young children (under the age of three) we found that most believe that gremlins and goblins and fantastic creatures actually live inside The Box, where they can be called forth by means of a handheld remote-control device!

TV is a seeing-and-hearing experience only. It denies the doing of life. And what it pictures is real to a child, but not real in comparison to the rest of the world.

Teaching through Modeling

Modeling is a key to understanding how TV affects children.

A child doesn't automatically arrive in the world saying "please" and "thank you." Neither does a child feel gentleness and kindness as a first reaction to others. Sensitivity to others doesn't develop spontaneously either. All of these behaviors are learned.

Sensitive behavior must be modeled for the child, who must then try it out. If the child's behavior is rewarded, the behavior is reinforced in a positive way. This is repeated until the child has become conditioned to the behavior, and it is exhibited almost as a habitual response.

The pattern becomes one of modeling (watching a behavior), doing (trying out the behavior), and reward/punishment (reinforcing or changing the behavior). Educators often call this three-step process training.

Training deals with the will. It is effective only if the child perceives that authority is involved in the instruction. It is linked primarily to repetition, including repeated rewards or punishments. It is deeply rooted in doing. It is also the most effective, most consistent, and longest-lasting way to learn. One of the most famous proverbs concerns training: "Train up a child in the way he should go, and when he is old he will not depart from it" (Prov. 22:6).

What happens, however, if the doing phase is mostly eliminated? The learning process then becomes much more like a communication exercise processed solely in the mind. The doing is replaced by mental rehearsal.

In most communication models, thought becomes expressed or encoded as a message, which is depicted as being sent from a sender to a receiver through some type of channel. The receiver then provides feedback to the sender.

The person receiving the message decodes it so that it has meaning, or thought, for her. Decoding is possible because of previous knowledge, and it is influenced by the sum of a receiver's habits, attitudes, and biases.

The communication process is considered accurate and complete to the extent that the encoded message matches the decoded message. In other words, the dog in the mind of Person A looks, wags its tail, and barks like the dog in the mind of Person B.

How does this relate to children and television? Children use the messages they receive in the first few years of their lives to form their most basic decoding abilities. Messages to them, therefore, carry a great deal more weight or impact than the same messages might carry to an adult.

Messages that are repeated carry the greatest weight. Whether it's a parent saying, "Don't do that" or "I love you," the child picks up the message and stores it. Repeated sayings become standards by which future behavior will be judged and, eventually, a template by which future behavior will be exhibited.

The loop of feedback is critical to the child. He'll test most messages to make sure he has them right. A child is going to question and question and question, which is his way of gathering information as much as it is a test of wills.

The direct results for such feedback are higher IQ and other test scores for children. In other words, children who don't get adequate feedback don't learn as quickly or as accurately as children who get plenty of feedback.

How does TV communicate to children? To be sure, TV provides messages—lots of them.

Adults receive those messages and tend to classify them as stories or as commercials. Young children, however, can't make that distinction. They haven't received enough messages yet. To them, everything appears to be a story.

Adults see a person pull out a gun and shoot another person, and they know that the person shot doesn't really die and that such violence is only a slice of life. Young children don't know that. They see the gun used as a way of dealing with a situation. They don't know that all conflicts aren't resolved in that manner.

And the examples could go on. The point is that children process messages generally in the same way adults do, but since they have received fewer messages in their lives, each message has greater weight and greater impact, and the messages they receive in abundance early in life are the messages they use as a baseline of information for evaluating future messages.

During my last eight years of talking to parents about their children and studying the effects of TV on them, this is the number-one stumbling block I've discovered: Adults, who have developed a sense of separating reality from fantasy, cannot fathom that children are incapable of thinking abstractly, that what children see is real to them.

Parents tend to look at the animated characters on TV and laugh them away as unreal and, therefore, fantasy. They believe their children see these characters in the same way. That simply is not the case.

Until a child is seven years old, he sees TV as reality. He views everything in a literal sense. In fact, until a child is seven or eight, he has little ability to think abstractly or to solve a problem in his head. Up until that time, most children solve problems with the aid of concrete helps, such as counting on their fingers and toes.

When I was two years old, I could hardly wait each week to see my hero, Lassie. I recall vividly one episode in which Lassie entered a burning barn to save its occupants. Suddenly the episode ended, and TO BE CONTINUED flashed on the screen.

I burst into tears. I was 100 percent convinced that my hero was, at that very moment, turning into a crispy critter. I would not be consoled until my father faked a call to the TV makers who knew Lassie and who conveyed that Lassie was still alive and well. It was several years before I realized that my father had faked that call.

No matter how much a parent tries to explain to a child that what he sees on TV isn't real, the child simply doesn't have the developmental capabilities to comprehend that information. He may say back to a parent, "It isn't real," but that only means the child has good parroting abilities.

What about feedback? Television doesn't provide any. No other activity in a child's life permits so much intake while demanding so little response. The child truly becomes a passive recipient of TV's messages.

By watching and hearing what's on TV, children are learning at three levels simultaneously. At the first level, children are learning a variety of skills, behaviors, attitudes, and information from a program.

The bulk of what they are learning, however, relates to how to think and how to act: how to commit crimes; how to inflict pain; how to ignore the needs of others; what products are worth buying; which people are considered sexually attractive.

At the second level, children are learning to see that information comes in sets between commercial breaks. Those sets have their own beginnings, middles, and endings. They are learning a way to think, a learning set.

At the third level, children are learning many symbolic codes. They are learning the syntax of television. They are becoming excellent readers of visual cues.

We'll deal with each level in greater depth later in the book. For now, however, we can draw the conclusion that the primary teaching and learning method employed by television—in the absence of doing and in the absence of feedback or reinforcement—is to model behavior repeatedly.

Teaching through Repetition

Repetition is the primary way TV teaches. TV gets a child's attention, shows behavior, then repeats attention-getting devices and behaviors.

Some devices used by TV aren't necessarily bad in and of themselves. Children learn by means of music, rhyme, simple narratives, and visual stimuli —including animation—apart from TV. We teach our children nursery rhymes and sing little songs to them and, in the process, give them familiarity with their language and encourage the development of memory. We speak to children in simple sentences.

But other messages that come by way of TV again and again are not beneficial, and we need to be vitally aware that repetition reinforces those messages just as effectively. We also need to be aware that nowhere is the compounded effect of repetition more prominent than on Saturday morning television.

The learning effects achieved through repetition take hold early. Researchers at the Queen's University in Belfast, Northern Ireland, noticed that infants whose mothers had been faithful soap-opera viewers during pregnancy suddenly stopped crying and came to attention when the theme music of their mothers' favorite soap opera began playing. Children who were not born to soap-opera-watching mothers kept right on crying. Television's influence may even seep through the uterine wall!

Infants as young as ten months are able to learn from what they see on television. Researchers have found that children begin to pay consistent attention to TV programs about the age of two, and that TV begins to exert influence on a child's life at the age of three years.

Three types of repetition are prevalent on Saturday mornings.

The first is the repetition of programs. "Mister Rogers" has been around long enough now to have chalked up 570 shows, with only about 15 new episodes introduced each year. Most shows are reruns or reruns of reruns. Their content and styles of clothing and hairdos are outdated; yet they go on and on.

In children's programming, a series is generally ordered by cycles, usually thirteen to seventeen episodes scheduled over a two-year period. This means that an episode will be aired approximately six to eight times on a network as part of one cycle. If the series is popular, the network might ask for several new episodes. If the series is not popular, it is generally not renewed, and these episodes are usually turned over to a syndication company, which sells them to local stations, cable channels, and outlets overseas.

Of course, after a few years, a new batch of children has come along, so the reruns can actually be rerun again to a virtually new audience. Few modifications are required since animated characters can be updated visually much more cheaply than if the entire series needed to be reshot with new narration. Examples of these series include "Archie," "Woody Woodpecker," "Rocky and Bullwinkle," "Casper the Friendly Ghost," "Mr. Magoo," and "Mighty Mouse."

When a program is especially popular, the networks look for spin-off possibilities, or taking one character from the old show and building a new show around him or her. Of course, many animated segments from the old show can and will be used again in the new one.

Anniversaries are major times for cartoon characters to reappear.

"Paddington Bear" and "The Chipmunks" both celebrated their thirtieth birthdays; "Mickey Mouse," "Charlie Brown," and the "Peanuts" gang, their fortieth; "Bugs Bunny," "Snow White," and "Superman," their fiftieth.

Some shows come back with a slight variation, such as "The New Archies," "The New Gidget," and "Popeye and Son," which were among the offerings that appeared on Saturday morning in 1988. Among the current repeats is "Mighty Mouse: The New Adventures."

Another recurring personage is "Captain Kangaroo." The Captain is still Bob Keeshan, who first appeared in our homes by means of TV on October 3, 1955, the same day that "The Mickey Mouse Club" premiered.

The second type of repetition prominent in children's programming is a repetition of characters from one show to the next and frequently from one format or viewing time period to the next. Some examples are "Dennis the Menace," "Robocop," and "Droids: The Adventures of R2D2 and C3PO."

A number of animated children's shows in the recent past have been take-offs of programs originally scheduled for prime time. "The Oddball Couple" was such a spin-off derived from "The Odd Couple." The nighttime "Kung Fu" spun itself into "Hong Kong Phooey" on Saturday morning. "Gilligan's Island" became the "Adventures of Gilligan" on Saturday morning.

In nearly all cases, the adult nighttime version came first.

The parents who are viewers of the nighttime programs tend to give their support to and even encourage their children to watch the animated series on which these programs are based. The parents are often unaware, however, that the animated version has far more violence than the nighttime program. The same holds true for animated series that are spin-offs of popular PG–rated movies, which many parents allow, and even encourage, their preteens to see.

Characters never die. They become franchised and move into new formats and new time zones. Characters repeat as much as programs do.

A third type of repetition in children's programming is that of content. A high percentage of children's programs have the same basic plot lines depicting the same general characterizations. The scripts seem almost recycled, with a change of faces, voices, and character identities to confuse the innocent.

Sometimes the changes aren't even camouflaged. For example, Daffy Duck, Bugs Bunny, Porky Pig, Sylvester, and Tweety became the "Quackbusters" for Warner Home Video. Not much of a leap from "Ghostbusters," and even less a leap in content.

Why so much repetition? Because children don't mind. Children learn by doing something again and again. They read their books dozens, even hundreds, of times and never seem to weary of their favorite ones.

A strength of "Sesame Street" is that it presents a concept in a variety of ways, again and again. Repetition is a key to learning for children. It's the key to understanding children's television.

So What's a Parent to Do?

Recognize that TV is not a playmate or an entertainer nearly so much as it is a teacher for your child. Your child can't tell the difference between make-believe and fantasy on The Box. The messages that come over a TV set are reinforced because they are repeated and repeated. They spawn mental rehearsal; repetition substitutes for feedback. As such, the messages of television become engrained in a child's memory patterns through a process of attention getting, modeling, and repetition. The program, the characters, and the story lines are all repeated and repeated.

Repetition is the key to learning. Repetition is the key to brainwashing.

The critical questions are these: What messages are being repeated? Is your child hearing messages that you want to have reinforced?

Chapter Three

The Omnipresent Storyteller

Stories shape the minds of children.

—Socrates

Go into any high school and see how limited the students' perception of themselves is, how crippled their imagination, how unable to tell a story, to read and concentrate, or even to describe an event accurately a moment after it happens. See how easily they are bored, how quickly they take up the familiar reclining position in the classroom, how short their attention span is.

—Novelist Jerzy Kosinski

Much of school learning is aimed at the development of four major skills: language acquisition and use, reasoning or thinking ability, problem-solving ability, and creativity. A major way in which children learn those skills is through the vehicle of stories.

Stories have long been the most powerful vehicle for passing information from generation to generation. They have been used to teach ethics, history, and literature.

Stories are central to religious thought and feeling and are the conveyors of values and ideals. They provide a mirror for life and, therefore, a vehicle for analyzing life. The average person will see some 30,000 electronic stories before he or she reaches the age of twenty-one.

What kind of storyteller is TV? What does TV do to a child's development of language, reasoning ability, problem-solving skills, and creativity?

Television as a Language Teacher

Children are born into a world where everyone speaks what amounts to a foreign language. The only way to learn that language is to hear it spoken, then to hear it and hear it some more.

Think about it. Much of what a child hears during his preschool years takes on the quality of a story. Mother explains, "Now we're going to take a bath," and the subsequent story involves dirt and toes and soapsuds. Mother doesn't know she's telling a story, but she is. Dad comes home and tells the story about his day. Grandma stops by and tells the story of a stuffed animal.

Story and dialogue and the format of drama all help children learn their language. They develop an ear for words. On television, the stories have a visual component. Children begin to learn a visual language that results in an eye for shapes and colors and fashions. As surely as their bodies store food, their minds store the images of TV dramas not only in their minds but as their minds.

What is the language of Saturday morning television? It is a predominantly visual language, far out of proportion to the world at large, based on motion and laughter, with few words and simplistic plots. The vocabulary is aimed at a three-year-old level, even though children's programming is generally considered to cover ages two to eleven.

Nearly 80 percent of Saturday morning shows are animations. More than 15 hours of animated films and cartoons are aired every Saturday morning, and more than 10,000 hours of animated programming are available in the syndicated TV market.

Why animation? For several reasons, all of them related to money.

The Federal Communications Commission released a study titled "The Economics of Network Children's Television" in 1972. The study, conducted by Alan Pearce, explored in detail the costs and revenues of children's programming. They found that the cost of producing a weekend cartoon show ran between $10,000 and $11,000 per half hour (assuming that the shows repeated six times in two years). Shows for children featuring dramatic action and airing during prime time cost $250,000 per hour or $125,000 per half hour. Even though the FCC report is fairly old, the proportions remain similar in today's dollars. Cartoons are ten times cheaper to produce than live drama!

Cartoons

The birthday of animated cartoons is considered to be June 12, 1913, when J. R. Bray's "The Artist's Dream" was released by Pathe. The central character was a dachshund, and many people have titled the cartoon "The Dachshund." It ran at Clune's Theater in 1913, and viewers rated it hysterically funny.

Virtually all the early cartoons were drawn to create a visual joke. Some pictures were very short, such as "How a Mosquito Operates," which was only 600 feet long. Some of the story lines were as simple as a man rolling his eyes and blowing smoke from his cigar at the passing of a pretty girl, or a dog jumping through a hoop. And most had very simple animation techniques, generally only one or two moving parts.

When Disney premiered "Steamboat Willie," the first Mickey Mouse picture, on September 19, 1928, a new level of animation emerged. Mickey Mouse was fully animated; all parts of the screen and the mouse had motion. But the story lines remained simple ones rooted in visual jokes beyond anything that could be real.

These early animations were aimed at adults first. Adults were the primary theater-goers in the early days of film. Taking their cue from vaudeville, the short features and animated features were novelties, tricks, and opening acts intended to loosen up the audience.

The advantages of animation for the network executive today are twofold. First, the programs can be produced by low-priced technical processes rather than high-priced artistic or live-action processes. The producer can employ a cast of thousands to do incredible stunts with a minimal amount of money. Second, animations tend to transcend time since they are far less subject to sociocultural and fashion trends, and that can mean endless syndication.

From a director's standpoint, animation allows for a maximum amount of preplanning and a minimum amount of human foible. Human temperament; weather; the time of day; and location—all can be overcome readily.

Animation was once considered an art as well as a craft. Painstaking care went into the 24 drawings required for each frame of film. Today, using computer techniques, the sequences often are based on 8,000 to 10,000 drawings per episode. Many sequences are kept as stock and reused, such as chase sequences and background scenes. Technicians can break down a visual message into component bits and later reassemble a new visual using that glance, that arm motion, or that tree once again. The animation is back to a fewer-parts-moving format, also; while the lips of an animated character may move, the rest of the face seldom shows motion.

Today's cartoons, though heavily emphasizing visual language and visual components, actually have very little visual content. The subliminal message is sent that the margins for variation in this world are fixed. Color values, certain outline shapes, the range of mobility, and other visual images recorded in the computer's memory banks form the definitive pool of imagery that will bombard a child month after month and year after year. Over time, children are seeing a visual message that is more homogenous, more mechanical, less artistic, and less varietal than the cartoons of even two decades ago. One might go so far as to say they are less visually creative.

In the end, lack of words may be the most damaging trait of cartoons. Some researchers have hypothesized that children who watch a great deal of TV are developing the nonverbal, visual hemisphere of their brains at the expense of developing the other hemisphere in which words and logic reside.

Constant motion compounds the effect of the heavy reliance on visual cues. Anyone who watches Saturday morning television for four straight weeks might draw at least one conclusion: life is a chase scene.

"Pac-Man," the series based on the video game, is solely about chasing and chomping. Not much of a plot line.

The "Go-Bots" cartoon is one of the most violent, simplistic, boring, and poorly animated cartoon series I've reviewed. The underscore of music and sound effects is nonstop. I could find nothing redemptive or artistic about the series. I could discern only one overriding concept: action.

Humor

Most adults assume that animated programs are funny to children. Yet most children actually find little to laugh at.

Perhaps that's why animated programs are almost always underscored with nonstop music and sound effects. Even the producers can't figure out where to put laugh-track inserts!

Dramatic programs, especially situation comedies (known more popularly as sitcoms), use the laugh track, however. In fact, every sitcom uses a laugh track today. The laff-track, as it is called, provides positive reinforcement even when an enemy is being shot out of the air with a cosmic ray gun or flattened by a steamroller.

The laugh track was pioneered during "The Hank McCune Show" in 1950. Its subsequent and increasing use has led to the development of a social policy for shaping the public's sense of humor. If a show's producers think something is funny, they engineer laugh-track reinforcement to ensure that the whole nation will think it's funny. When and how do we teach our children to boo what is occult, obscene, ingratiating, or boring?

Which jokes are being legitimized? Those rooted in slapstick, the drop-your-pants, pie-in-the-face actions. Rarely if ever can you find a joke rooted in wordplays, visual images, or musical oddities on programs created for young children.

But, you may ask, can young children appreciate more subtle jokes? Definitely! Children frequently respond with spontaneous laughter in nonmedia situations to what someone said or how something looked as much as to what someone did. Perhaps one of the best parts of the "Captain Kangaroo" program is the Captain's great love of language and his humorous stringing together of words and phrases.

Humor traditionally has been rooted in human foible. We sometimes laugh when someone trips or spills hot coffee, even though we try not to laugh! In virtually all cases, humor is also related to the concept of surprise or the unexpected. We laugh because someone responds in a way that we hadn't anticipated. That was the entire formula for "Candid Camera"!

The humor in cartoons today is quite different. More often than not, it is rooted in insult and injury. Our children see horror and slime as being funny, because horror and slime are held up to be funny and engineered to appear funny.

Drama

Many of today's children's programs are not intended to tell funny stories. They are dramas, not comedies. In fact, most TV is written in a dramatic mode, even many of the animated series on Saturday mornings.

Drama is always about conflict. That key fact cannot be overemphasized. News shows, advertisements, and political announcements are all shaped by that structure.

Bugs Bunny and the farmer, Sylvester and Tweety, Roadrunner and Coyote—these are all classic dynamic-duo dramas that children can understand. A child, too, competes for space, objects, and attention against other children, an adult, or an older sibling. One-to-one conflict is the drama of a child.

Today's myths, however, are rooted in the conquest of an entire world or planet, or even of a galaxy or the universe. The conflict is between groups of people or teams, as it were. The young child doesn't operate on that frequency yet.

To hold the attention of an adult audience, the dramatic conflict must evoke intense human feelings. These feelings often are out of the range of the child.

What happens once emotions are piqued? As soon as viewers find their intellectual curiosity awakened; or are gripped by fear or anxiety, or respond with feelings of love or hate, terror, revulsion, or rage, they are delivered to the commercials. Reactions that have been engaged are abruptly disengaged. Given these constant interruptions, emotions that may readily build into a climax on the movie screen rarely have a chance to develop on TV. A child thus rides an emotional roller coaster, and it's a roller coaster that he's too short to ride according to the yardstick measurement at the ride's entrance.

Music and Other Techniques

To heighten the intensity of drama, and sometimes on Saturday mornings just to attempt to retain a child's attention, a program often is underscored with music from start to finish.

Consider for a moment the musical language that accompanies children's cartoons. Most of it is based on tunes with 32 bars in 4/4 time and orchestrated with a limited range of instruments. The music is just as cheap as the illustration technique. And in some shows ("Jem," "The Droids"), rock music plays a role.

The purpose of music, to a great extent, is to create emotion artificially. If children are incapable of understanding the scope and emotional cues aimed at heightening the dramatic effect, perhaps they can be aroused at the most basic levels through music!

In many cases, camera techniques are designed to be intense, even if they are not violent or sexual in nature. Intensity in films and on TV is created through pace and the use of extreme close-ups and/or unusual camera angles. Add high-contrast lighting techniques and you have what psychologist Bruno Bettelheim calls an "authoritarian nature" to the program.

Children begin to expect certain things out of certain blocks of time. They anticipate certain skills or content at the presence of a song, for example. "The Real Ghostbusters" animated series does a good job of this type of reinforcement. The minute the ghostbusting crew is about to take action, one hears the catchy rhythmic theme music.

Dr. Mary Alice White, a professor at Teachers College of Columbia University, has said,

> By the time they are three or four years old, children have learned that music and sound effects, and sometimes changes in types of voices, are cues to make them look at a TV screen. They come to school with a set of strategies they have learned from the electronic system that do not apply to the classroom setting. I don't think they know when to listen.

How frustrating it must be for teachers to stand in front of a classroom of students that expect them to perform and to be as entertaining as what they have seen a few hours before on TV! How frustrating not to get the attention of students who are waiting for a music underscore to tell them which facts are important.

Distortion of Time

Where does this pattern of learning sets lead? First, children become accustomed to a break in information every few minutes. Concentration is limited to twenty-minute time frames. Problems generally are resolved within a program—some within thirty minutes, some within sixty minutes and, on Saturday mornings, most within eight minutes!

Actually, the entire concept of an hour is distorted by TV, especially on Saturday mornings. "Sesame Street," for example, is based on a 54-minute hour, the remainder given over to commercial messages. For the rest of television, the 50.5-minute hour seems acceptable for prime time, the 44-minute hour acceptable for daytime dramas and talk shows. The 60-second commercial has been joined by the 20- and 30-second varieties, not to mention the split commercials that wrap around companion commercials during a break.

The nightly news has only 21.5 minutes of news during a 30-minute slot. The other 8.5 minutes are devoted to commercials. That means nearly a quarter of the time is being spent on commercial watching. Furthermore, the average length of a network news story is 30 seconds, the length of a commercial! We are basing, to a great extent, our national understanding of the world on commercial-length bits of information, since 67 percent of Americans say they get most of their news from TV and nearly 50 percent think TV is the most credible news medium.

Educators have long had fears about television's effect on a child's attention span. Most formal educational studies have done little to confirm those fears, though. One study by Salomon (1974) found that children who watched a fast-paced TV program then had difficulty persisting in a tedious school-like task. Anecdotal evidence from teachers varies. This conclusion seems to be most likely: television does little to enhance the attention span of a child. Children who begin with low attention spans are affected most.

Again and again teachers point to a lack of tolerance in students who are heavy TV watchers, perhaps a more critical issue than that of attention span. Children who watch TV may well be able to attend to information, but they show a remarkable lack of persistence and patience when asked to wait, to complete a task requiring multiple tries, or to engage in a task that has several stages or levels. They expect all problems to be solved and all projects to be completed within thirty to sixty minutes, maximum!

One kindergarten teacher noted,

> Many children come to school revved up . . . totally overstimulated from their morning dose of the tube. . . . They can't sit still; they can't focus or follow directions. Hyperactivity goes hand in hand with the inability to concentrate on anything for very long. And if you can't get them to focus, you can't get them to think and learn. (95:52)

The rhythms and cadence of society have been dramatically fragmented, and when time is shortened, the content must, by necessity, be simplified. Television leaves little room for complexity, and that is especially true for Saturday morning programs.

News programs deliberately avoid providing context, which is necessary to make sense of the events reported. On the evening news, about two dozen topics are touched upon in as many minutes; indiscriminately jostling up against each other are announcements of war efforts and peace efforts, earthquakes and football scores, beauty pageants and rocket launches. Any interest in one story is immediately squelched by the next bit of information's arriving on the screen. At the conclusion of most news programs, it's difficult to recall more than five or six segments.

The plot lines of Saturday morning take on the same character. No context. Little explanation or background. No discussion. No interpretation. Just the action, ma'am, and on to the commercials.

This approach to giving and receiving information assumes that the viewer has the ability to scan a data bank, process the facts, calculate alternative outcomes, and reason things through to a conclusion, all of which assumes training, skill, knowledge, intellect, and control. These are qualities not many adults, and virtually no young children, possess.

We are asking a child to take oversimplified slices of information, prioritize them, and provide context for them. A child simply cannot do that. He doesn't have enough experience, information, or intellectual development. How can a child understand the importance of a water shortage or a flood when he has never experienced either? And on Saturday mornings, how can a child know that different motivations might give rise to different behaviors?

How do children develop reasoning skills? Largely through talking. A child must express himself to develop a true ability to think through problems. Some schools today are finding it highly beneficial to have children dictate stories to their teachers before they can read or write by themselves. These first attempts at composition are important motivators for language-skill learning, and they also help children learn to separate fantasy from reality in their thought processes. Above all, they help children think through a story from start to finish.

Educators also repeatedly report that when children work together on a project, they solve problems more quickly. They are learning, in the process, to disagree, to take turns, to speculate, and to weigh various opinions and ideas. These skills aren't learned through lecture or by the autocratic telling of a story on TV.

A Ceiling on Creativity

Today's cartoons are not rooted in a child's imagination. They are grounded in the imagination of adults. They reflect an adult creativity and an adult knowledge both of the world and of language.

A young child, who has no knowledge of the world at large or the technology that has given birth to robots, doesn't imagine wars between competing forces of robots, or "Go-Bots," as the case may be.

Can blue jiggle? What color is the letter *A?* Can I explore in a picture? Why don't I see myself when I look into a daisy? These are the kinds of questions children ask. These are the questions that become the stuffing of creativity.

Cartoon animations answer these and similar questions for children quite literally. Blue does jiggle. Furthermore, squares turn into circles, "stones get up and dance . . . human figures shatter to pieces and are instantly reconstituted as the pieces pick themselves up and rejoin each other" (29:58–59). On TV, everything imaginative takes on a literal quality.

The greater harm may well be that TV eliminates the sense of boredom out of which creativity arises. Jerry Mander, author of *Four Arguments for the Elimination of Television,* tells about his childhood experiences without TV:

> I am a member of the pre-TV generation. Until I was 14 or 15 we had no television. And I can still remember what it felt like to come home every day. First, I'd go look in the kitchen or refrigerator to see if there were any special snacks my mother left for me. I'd take care of those. Then, slowly becoming bored, I'd play with the dog for a bit. Here comes the boredom. Nothing to do.

> Slowly, I'd slip into a kind of boredom that seemed awful. An anxiety
> went with it, and a gnawing tension in the stomach. It was exceedingly
> unpleasant, so unpleasant that I would eventually decide to act—to do
> something. I'd call a friend. I'd go outdoors. I'd go play ball. I'd read. I
> would do something.
>
> Looking back, I view that time of boredom, of "nothing to do," as the
> pit out of which creative action springs. Taking all young people to-
> gether, you could think of it as a kind of genetic pool of creativity. You
> get to the bottom of your feelings, you let things slip to their lowest
> ebb, and then you take charge of your life. Not wanting to stay in that
> place, you make an act. You experience yourself in movement, with
> ideas, in action.
>
> Nowadays, however, at the onset of that uncomfortable feeling, kids
> usually reach for the TV switch. TV blots out both the anxiety and the
> creativity that might follow. (43:4–5)

To develop their creative abilities, children need to talk to other
youngsters and to their parents and teachers. Children don't develop
creativity just by listening.

Children need to be active in their experiments and play. They
need to be doing freehand artwork, crafts, and building projects.

Above all, to develop creativity, as well as language, problem-
solving, and reasoning skills, children need to be read to. Reading
aloud to a child helps him hear the language. It helps her learn how
to manipulate words, which give rise to ideas.

In *The Gift of Child's Play,* Piers and Landau describe what happens
when a child hears a story read to him:

> In being read to or told a story, a child has to make up his own images
> about the people, events, scenes in the story. He brings them to life in
> his imagination. Moreover, he has considerable control over the pace
> and rhythm of the material presented. Children often ask an adult who
> is reading to them to go back and read something over, or to stop and
> talk about what is happening on the page. None of that is possible in
> watching television.

Well, you might conclude, TV may not help a child's language,
reasoning, problem-solving, or creative development, but does it really hurt a child?

In a two-year study, Williams (1977) found that increased exposure to TV was adversely and strongly related to a child's fluency

with words, as well as to his creativity. The reading skills of children who had started watching TV in grades four and five were much higher than those who had been watching TV since early childhood.

Research has also shown that children who are heavy viewers (more than four hours a day) put in less effort on schoolwork, have poorer reading skills, play less well with friends, and have fewer hobbies and activities than children who are not heavy viewers.

The heavy TV viewers sometimes forget to play. They also tend to jump from one toy to the next, creating a mess but not truly playing. They don't know how to play, and as a result, they can't benefit from all that play offers, including the development of their language abilities, the skills and persistence needed for problem solving, and the creativity gained through the creation of characters and plots.

Our conclusion? Television is a prolific but bad storyteller. It is too visually oriented. It moves too quickly and is based too much in dramatic emotions. It is too fragmented in time. It is too literal in presentation. And it is too omnipresent in most children's lives as the primary storyteller.

So What's a Parent to Do?

Choose slower-paced programs for your child to watch, for example, "Mister Rogers," a PBS production, which hit the airwaves in the 1960s. Things move slowly in Mister Rogers' neighborhood. The program's low-key style has been warmly received by children, who perceive Mister Rogers as their friend. The program is intensely personal, and the attitudes and behaviors demonstrated in both live vignettes and fantasy (through puppets and actors) emphasize cooperation, compassion, kindness, and empathy.

Studies have shown that children who watch this program show an increase in their ability to persist with a task, and that their increase is greater than children who watch aggressive cartoons or more neutral informational programming.

Emphasize books over TV. Literacy means more than knowing the alphabet. On virtually all programs, books are rarely portrayed as being a viable form of fun. A parent needs to counteract this book deprivation by promoting books, by reading books, and by reading books to a child. Give your child access to magazines, books, and maps. Make visiting the library a regular activity.

Watch TV with your child. A study reported in the *Christian Science Monitor* compared the creativity of four groups of children. One group watched TV alone, the second played alone, the third watched TV with an adult, and the fourth played with an adult. The highest levels of creativity were found in the third and fourth groups.

When you watch TV with your child, you can help your child understand the visual messages it conveys. You can point out meanings, give context, and help a child understand a character's motivation.

Use TV as a tool. Try add-on stories with your child. Ask, What do you think happened to this character, or these characters, next? What do you suppose happened as a result of the story we just saw? Get the child involved in making up a new plot.

We've found that when children make up stories, many times their stories will have happier endings than the ones they just saw. They can resolve some of the behavior they have seen by putting it in a story that includes their own growing sense of values.

You can also use TV to springboard into other activities and information. Find where the Cosby family lives on a map. Was there really a town named Paradise? Where exactly did the Pony Express young riders travel?

Children like detail work. They like to keep track of things, organize things, and make sense out of things. Ask your child to keep a journal about certain TV programs, listing what the characters did. Encourage your child to find patterns in their behavior.

Choose activities other than TV to promote learning skills. Children like to take walks. They enjoy being outdoors and exploring. Learn to play games with your child—board games, hide-and-seek, word games. Encourage pretend activities. Ask your child to build his own house in the corner of a room or a hallway. Ask your child to make up a play and to perform it for you.

Gail Hartzell, a teacher from Waterlook Schools in rural north-eastern Ohio, said in a Knight-Ridder newspaper column: "The [television] screen does it all—thinking for themselves has gone down the drain."

Don't let that be true for your child!

Chapter Four

How Did We Get Here from There?

In 1948, there were 250,000 TV sets in the world. Today there are more than 750 million.

The price of a midsize car in 1940 was $1,000 and a TV set was $660. Now, you can buy a midsize car for about $14,000 and a TV set for under $100.

Television provides access into more than 71 million homes in the United States.

Commercial stations account for about 85 percent of total broadcast hours.

In 1978, Earle Barcus of Boston University studied weekend and after-school programming. He found that educational programs were aired on network stations only 16 percent of the time for the time periods he studied. Most of the educational programs were funded by the federal government.

For the most part, Barcus found that the programs featured themes of crime, domestic affairs, love and romance, and science and technology. The most common format for children's programs was animation. Situation and family comedies were most popular on the independent stations.

How is it that TV has come to have that profile, which remains virtually unchanged more than a decade after the Barcus review? Consider how we got here from there.

Several basic concepts are at the root of what we see on TV today, the foremost that TV is a business. Its purpose from the other side of The Box is to make money, not to entertain, educate, or inform. Entertainment, education, and information are provided only to draw audiences in order to sell time. The better the entertainment and the more popular the show, the more the network or channel can charge for advertising time.

From its inception, TV in the United States was created to be a commercial vehicle and an instrument of advertising. It was assumed from the very beginning that every program would one day be subject to sale to sponsors.

During the first few years, however, the economic incentives of the industry were directed mainly toward market development. The industry needed viewers, which meant that Americans needed to own television sets. Programming was aimed, therefore, toward promoting the medium itself.

Children's programs were designed during this time specifically to attract a viewing audience. In 1951, the four networks (NBC, CBS, ABC, and DuMont, since defunct) aired twenty-seven hours of children's programming a week. Most programs were aired between 5 and 8 P.M. The networks developed a number of programs, such as "Howdy Doody" and "Kukla, Fran, and Ollie," live-action puppet shows. Other live-action shows for children included "Captain Video," "Hopalong Cassidy," and "Mr. I Magination."

Nearly half the children's programs at the network level were presented without advertiser sponsorship in those early years.

At the local level, stations were given time slots that the networks considered slightly less than desirable. Local stations aired inexpensive leftovers from the movie houses, including old animated short films. These offerings were intended to appeal to the mass audience.

Between 1949 and 1952, the number of TV sets in the U.S. jumped from 190,000 to more than 16 million. Television rapidly became an enviable advertising medium. The role of sponsors and advertising agencies was quickly defined.

The strength of a program to an advertiser was, and is, rooted in the number of eyes watching it. The advertisers became more sophisticated as the years passed, demanding specific eyes, such as all adults, men primarily, women primarily, children, and so forth.

Prime time became too valuable to be wasted on children's programming. The networks began to be less responsible for the creation of programming. Film series such as "I Love Lucy" were produced independently and sold to the networks, who could in turn sell them overseas at a later time for added revenue.

Locally, stations continued to offer old theatrical cartoons and short subjects. Surveys showed that the majority of the cartoon programs got high ratings; bad cartoons were preferred to bad dramatic shows or poorly produced local live programs.

In the mid-1950s, the networks looked more to Hollywood for the production of children's programming. "Captain Kangaroo" and

"Ding Dong School" were two shows that appeared then. In 1954, ABC scored a big hit with a new prime-time program called "Disneyland." It was a watershed program in that it was incredibly popular with sponsors, who clamored for more programs of that type with which to associate their names. The sponsors were attracted to the program's message and quality, not to the fact that the program was aimed at an audience of children. The "Mickey Mouse Club," a spin-off from the "Disneyland" program, was sponsored by companies *not* specializing in children's products.

Simultaneously, toy companies, which did very little advertising on TV in those days, experimented with manufacturing toys related directly to TV shows. The coonskin cap, related to the "Davy Crockett" show, was an early success story.

In the late 1950s, the networks gave the hours between four and seven P.M. to local stations. The interest of the networks lay almost exclusively between seven and eleven P.M., the prime-time hours with the big audience numbers. Almost overnight, network favorites such as "Mickey Mouse Club" and "Howdy Doody" became casualties.

In 1960, another watershed program hit the air: "The Flintstones," created by Hanna-Barbera and designed for family viewing. The networks realized that an animated series could be created specifically for TV.

At the same time, executives were waking up to the fact that children were influencing their parents' shopping habits! They quickly defined what they called the youth market, and they demanded programs on which to advertise their products directly to children. Nestle's Quick was only one such advertiser.

The networks again got into the business of producing children's programs, but more important, they moved to isolate a time block for children's programming. The choice? Saturday morning!

As early as the 1960s, commentators and educators referred to Saturday morning as the children's ghetto. The children's ghetto is considered to run from eight A.M. to noon every Saturday. The programs are primarily animations provided by only a handful of studios. An occasional variety show turns up or, even more rarely, an action-adventure series with children as actors.

Saturday morning programming is designed for three- to eleven-year-olds, according to a former director of children's programming at CBS, Allan Ducovny, although the Nielsen and Arbitron rating services generally consider the children's audience to be two to eleven years of age.

Plot lines, artistic mediums, and language of these programs are aimed at a low common denominator indeed—the preschooler. No network distinguishes between programs for the two to six and six to eleven age ranges, for example, even though educators underscore the vast differences in learning styles, humor, and language ability between these two age groupings.

About 16 percent of the time is allotted for commercials. Virtually all the programs on the air as of this writing are linked in what is often called a total marketing strategy to dolls (and their accompanying clothing, housing, weaponry, vehicles, and gear), storybooks, comic books, records, clothing, foods (including candy and vitamins), feature-length movies, video games, school supplies (from pencils to notebooks), and the list goes on. The word for it all? *Licensing.*

The networks settled on animation as the preferred format because it allowed them to produce shows at a cost that would still give them room for profit. The advertisers, while eager to reach the children's market, weren't willing to pay anything close to prime-time rates.

As I mentioned in an earlier chapter, animated programs could be produced for about one-tenth the cost of a live show. Furthermore, animated programs could be rerun more often, requiring fewer original shows per series. And the animated shows readily translated to foreign markets because they were virtually culture free. One need only dub in new audio to adapt "Bullwinkle and Rocky" to a Japanese audience.

Independent production companies followed the networks' lead. They grabbed onto the idea of producing programs that would play directly to the advertisers' desires. They helped create products related to the programs and the advertiser and then produced cartoons that featured those products. That approach secured their favor with the sponsors and also made them more appealing to the networks so that the work they produced might remain on the air longer.

As early as 1967, Joseph Barbera said,

We're doing monster stuff, mainly . . . comic-book fiction, super heroes, and fantasy. Not out of choice, you understand. It's the only
thing we can sell to the networks and we have to stay in business.

Commercial broadcasters look to audience ratings to determine
which programs to sponsor. Since the shows have pretty much a
two-year life cycle, advertisers are frequently signed up for new
programs even before a program airs. This has led to a reliance on
old techniques. If the old show plot lines and characters drew an
audience, the producer feels more confident that the new show will
also; the advertisers also gravitate toward this comfort zone. Once
something is established on Saturday morning, it's difficult to stem
the tide or to change formats.

What about Educational TV?

From the beginning, the purposes of commercial broadcasting
have frequently run crossways to those of educational producers.
For the most part, formal attempts at teaching by TV have failed in
the commercial marketplace.

The early puppet shows of the 1940s disappeared during World
War II, and the idea of educational TV didn't reappear until 1952,
when the FCC allocated 242 UHF channels for education, and the
Ford Foundation of the Educational Radio and Television Center
was established in 1958. The Ford Foundation entity later became
National Educational Television, or NET.

The problem with early educational TV efforts seems to have
followed a cycle: a lack of understanding of the medium by the
instructors, resulting in poorly conceived and poorly executed programs, which in turn failed to hold an audience, which in turn resulted in the programs' being less attractive to funders.

By 1960, the Russians had launched Sputnik, and most Americans
were deeply concerned that our educational system, and specifically
our science teaching, was lagging behind the world standard. Noted
educator Charles Siepmann wrote,

Education needs television, and that desperately. . . . Television, we
hold, while not the deus ex machina to solve the crisis, is one indis-
pensable tool that we can and must use to extricate ourselves from the

grave trouble we are in, but of which all too few still seem to be aware.(58:6)

To keep educational programs on the air, the government, or public broadcasting, had to get into the act.

Then came Children's Television Workshop, which recognized that TV of any type had to compete in the marketplace for sponsor dollars; thus it had to attract and hold an audience. "Sesame Street," the CTW's first major production, did that. It used TV techniques to sell its product, which just happened to be education.

"Sesame Street" went on the air the same year that astronaut Neil Armstrong stepped onto the moon's surface. Both events were deeply rooted in Americans' intense national desire to succeed.

Actually, much of TV is rooted in that desire—to succeed in finances, in relationships, in winning over evil, in having the good life. Whether it's at the level of Mr. Wilson's wanting peace and quiet from Dennis the Menace, or in Dino-Riders' wanting a safe haven from the Rulons, the issue at stake is ultimately the achievement of an improved quality of life. More than any other, that has been the message of television since its inception.

Following "Sesame Street" was "The Electric Company," public television's other successful big-audience series. Again, the program was designed to compete for the commercial market and to sell children the product of remedial reading skills. The show used computer animation, film, and technical effects to good advantage.

Both programs were pioneers in research as to how children learn from TV. One of the foremost advantages held by "Sesame Street" even today is the research conducted during its more than twenty years on the air that shows conclusively that the program is accomplishing its goals. The producers can show funders definitively that children are performing better on assessment tests after watching the program. Those who watch fewer hours will gain less than those who watch more. Younger children, who have more to learn, show greater gains than older children, and so forth. As a result, Children's Television Workshop has become the major recipient of government funds (the major funder of educational programs is the Office of Education) and, thereby, the foremost educational television producer in the United States today.

Children's Television as a Whole

The best children's programs usually involve experts in the study of children and not just educators, although educators are important for the theory and research background they bring to a production. Experts are parents and those who work regularly with children who may have special needs, such as children with handicapping conditions or minority-race children.

The best programs target a specific group. "Sesame Street," for example, was aimed strictly at three- to five-year-olds. "The Electric Company" was aimed at children with reading problems.

The best programs have a clear set of educational goals of what they want the child to do as a result of watching the show.

Educational programs will not be aired, however, if children don't watch them. Educators face the challenge not only of targeting their programs, basing them on sound research, offering solid content, and having well-defined goals, but also of making their programs entertaining.

By the late 1960s the vast majority of the first-run children's programs were being produced by fewer than ten companies. Only one, Children's Television Workshop, had education as a goal.

Production companies during the 1970s and 1980s played more toward the interests of the toy and product manufacturers, who in turn saw that the more their toys and products were featured on a program, the higher their sales soared. The networks were in an increasingly powerful position. They could pick and choose among the advertising bidders—toy, candy, breakfast food, and soft-drink manufacturers for the most part—and then turn around and conduct research on the viewing habits and subsequent buying habits of the youth market to substantiate their increase in rates. The higher the rates, the more the manufacturers demanded that their products be promoted not only between segments of a program but also as the stars of the program.

By the late 1970s, advertisers spent nearly $400 million a year to convince children to buy their products. Today, nearly $700 million is spent. Advertisers who talk about a $50 billion market see that as a reasonable price to pay.

Advertisers have discovered several things through their marketing research. First, children, especially younger children, like loud, bright, and action-oriented commercials.

Second, children watch commercials if the commercials are similar in content and tone and, even more so, if similar in characters to the programs in which the commercials are embedded. Basically, the children's concentration isn't broken.

Third, children of different ages tend to watch TV at different times. Before nine A.M. on Saturdays, two- to five-year-olds control the dial; six- to eleven-year-olds prefer nine to ten A.M.; after that, the twelve-year-olds take over.

Fourth, children are good lobbyists for adult products.

Fifth, a miracle worker is the best hard-hitting spokesman for children. The superhero can demonstrate a food product or a household cleanser as well as he can a toy!

Furthermore, children can be sold on the value of almost anything. Useless toys hidden in cereal boxes are more valuable to small children than new cars. Their sense of value hasn't been developed. Under the age of five or so, they are highly impractical, open to suggestions, and fickle.

The two selling techniques that work best with children soon became obvious. Offer something for free; a child understands free. A child also responds to a commercial in which the product is shown to be popular with other children.

Thus the advertising formula became fairly set:

- Advertise your product with a superhero
- on a program featuring the superhero
- with lots of slam-bang action and color,
- offer something free,
- show happy kids with the product,
- place your message in the right hour or half-hour time slot,
- and above all, encourage the children to press mom or dad to buy the product for them the next time they go to the store!

Many of these threads came together in a powerful way in 1983 when the entire concept of superhero took on a new dimension: "He-Man and Masters of the Universe" hit the screen. It was a program with everything: it had superheroes; it was designed to sell toys to children; it showed lots of action; and it aired at the right time. But that time wasn't on Saturday morning!

The networks rejected "He-Man and Masters of the Universe" as being too violent. Undaunted, the creators of the show looked to the syndicated market, found a time slot on weekday afternoons and, in so doing, launched a new trend.

The Saturday morning cartoons based on toy products reached a high in 1986 with seventy such programs available to viewers in various markets. By 1988, the number had dropped to six. Where did the programs go? They followed "He-Man" to weekday afternoons.

In 1985, only eighteen children's shows were syndicated. By 1987, the number had nearly doubled to thirty-five. With more latch-key kids—children who come home from school, let themselves in the house, and often hear from their working parents to "watch TV and heat up a pizza until I get home"— the three to five P.M. market rapidly became more popular as a time slot for children.

Along with the number of shows came a larger audience, of course (52.5 total rating points in 1987 compared to only 43.2 points two years earlier), but because of the number of shows, each one actually had a smaller share of the market. To carve out a niche in the competition, the programs needed to feature more action, including more violence, a trend discussed in greater detail in a later chapter.

Two other significant things happened in the mid-1980s. In 1985, 20.6 percent of U.S. homes had videocassette recorders. Two years later the percentage was 44.1 percent, and it is now well over 50 percent. At the same time, cable penetration across the nation increased, and three viable cable channels were made available to children: Nickelodeon, TBS, and USA network.

Strip programming, 65 half hours aired Monday through Friday, became the norm for several years as a response to the new cable outlets available. The trend as of this writing is moving away from strip programming, with greater experimentation in the placement of programs. "Jem," "Visionaries," "The Comic Strip," and "Hanna-Barbera's Wonderful World" all have been thirteen-part series scheduled to air on weekends only. The content of the shows is connected to tell a broader story, with characters and plot lines carrying over from episode to episode.

Some marketers are trying five-part miniseries, airing during one week only. "The Adventures of the Teenage Mutant Ninja Turtles" first aired in this manner.

Live-action game shows, featuring children and aimed at children, are being introduced for the after-school market. "Double Dare" and "Funhouse," aired in 1988, were among the first.

ABC is pursuing "After School Specials," a series that initially took three years to develop and had a $1 million budget.

Meanwhile, children's programming aimed at delivering information or news has declined among the network offerings. CBS's "In the News" and ABC's "Schoolhouse Rock" were taken off the air because they failed to attract enough viewers and, therefore, failed to attract advertisers.

Most support for educational programming comes from the Office of Education, both at state and at national levels. The bulk of those funds continues to go to Children's Television Workshop and to the Emergency School Aid Act (ESAA) within the Office of Education, which then distributes the money to various production companies. ESAA money is allocated for programs that promote multicultural understanding and is limited to specific age levels and to certain categories of content.

Today approximately one hundred hours of network programming is scheduled each week aimed at children's viewing time.

The children's population is currently growing at a rate of 4 to 5 percent per year.

The Educational Testing Service projects that a child will have seven different careers during his lifetime.

The questions we need to ask are these: Do children have a choice of quality today or only a choice of quantity? Are programs today preparing children for the world they will face in the future? And most important, what are the goals of the program producers?

So What's a Parent to Do?

Be aware that TV is a business. At the same time, be aware that, as businesses, commercial broadcast stations have been licensed specifically as public trustees charged with certain responsibilities to serve the public interest and to develop programs that meet the needs and interests of children rather than those of merchants who sell to and through children.

William Melody raises these questions:

> Should special protections be provided to insulate children from direct advertising designed to stimulate their consumption desires so that they would become active lobbyists for the merchandiser within the family?
>
> Should public policy recognize a responsibility to provide a minimal level of programming on commercial stations specifically directed to the needs and interests of children?(46:4)

A further question might be asked, as was asked by Burth, a former chairman of the Federal Communications Commission: Can a commercial broadcasting system serve quality programs for children?

As a parent, you have a privilege and a responsibility to express your opinions and answers to these questions to the networks, to advertisers, and to your senators and representatives.

You must always recognize that your child is being taught by TV corporations. TV is a corporate-based school that operates according to a profit motive. In no period of history has the business community exerted so much educational influence on children as it does now.

Ask yourself frequently: What is the goal of this program? What is it teaching? What are its foremost educational goals?

You as a parent or concerned citizen must decide if you like today's trends or if you want to do something to change them.

PART
2
The Lessons

Young Child sits in front of The Box as a student sits in front of a teacher.

Today's lesson is violence. The Box will teach you how to punch, kick, and fight and that aggression is the prime means of resolving conflict. Never mind, Young Child, that the world operates differently.

Tomorrow's lesson involves social studies. The Box will present the world as it is perceived by television producers-to-be. Be aware, Young Child, that what you learn won't translate into real life.

The Box will also include lessons about sexuality and about drugs. We hope, Young Child, that you will ignore these messages. Nevertheless, they are part of the curriculum.

The Box will teach you how to shop, what to choose, and what is in. At least, Young Child, The Box will teach you what it has been paid to teach you, and along the way, you'll get an education in consumerism and materialism.

Finally, The Box will teach you religion. It probably won't teach you the religion that your parents are trying to teach you, Young Child, but never mind. You'll get hours of instruction free of charge, and that will more than offset the few minutes of Sunday school, church, synagogue, or other catechism that your parents offer. You'll be adept at recognizing and manipulating occult symbols and techniques, and Eastern religions will seem like second nature to you.

All of this education with free tuition is from The Box.

Get ready, Young Child. School is in session!

Chapter Five

The Ol' Sockeroo

In one segment of "The Go-Bots," the evil character Cy-Kill concludes, "Isn't mayhem wonderful?"

> *We but teach*
> *Bloody instructions, which, being*
> *taught, return*
> *to plague the inventor.*

—William Shakespeare

Through TV, we Americans are teaching violence to our children to an extent that no young people in any other nation, or at any other time in history, have been taught violence.

In 1954, violence-saturated action and adventure programming accounted for only 17 percent of prime-time network offerings. By 1960, the number had jumped to 60 percent.

Prior to the 1956–57 TV season, no more than one crime program had been among the top 20 programs in any year, according to Nielsen ratings.

By 1964, however, more than 200 hours of network TV per week were devoted to crime stories, with more than 500 killings committed each season. That represented a 90 percent increase in the level of crime scenes on TV since 1952.

In 1968, the National Association for Better Broadcasting estimated that a child between the ages of five and fifteen would watch the violent destruction of more than 13,400 persons (including animated characters) on TV.

Today a child will see 18,000 murders enacted on TV by the time he is sixteen. During his entire life, he will see more than 50,000 murders.

Nearly 70 percent of all programs aired during the family viewing hours of seven to nine P.M. have violence.

During children's viewing hours, nine out of ten programs have violent scenes. Given the number of incidents of violence, children's programming is five times more violent than prime-time shows.

Taking prime-time and weekend daytime hours together, four out of five programs show violent acts. Two-thirds of all major characters get involved in violent or aggressive actions.

The National Coalition on Television Violence, founded in 1980, considers more than ten acts of violence per hour to be highly violent. Most network Saturday morning cartoons average seventeen violent acts per hour, which is more than twice the number per hour during prime time.

Some episodes of the "Bugs Bunny Show" average more than 40 violent acts per hour. By the way, the most popular Saturday morning cartoon among preschoolers is still "Bugs Bunny & Tweety." The current "Teenage Mutant Ninja Turtles" animated series averages 34 violent acts an hour.

The "Roadrunner" cartoons were considered too violent in their day. They averaged nine to eleven aggressive acts per half hour. Consider the average rates for some of today's programs during a 20- to 22-minute "half-hour" segment:

"He-Man"	37 violent acts
"Dungeons and Dragons"	67 violent acts
"G.I. Joe"	80 violent acts
"Voltron"	84 violent acts
"Captain Power and the Soldiers of the Future"	124 violent acts

"Miami Vice" had only four to six violent acts per half hour!

By 1969, a violent episode was taking place every two minutes on the average for all Saturday morning cartoon programming, factoring in commercial time and the least violent programs. The average cartoon hour had nearly six times the violence rate of the average adult TV hour. That trend has held steady during the past twenty years.

Does it matter that TV, especially children's programming, is rooted in violence to this extent?

Research in the 1930s concluded that violence in movies had a marked effect on adolescents (Charters 1933). Later, comic strips that depicted violent or aggressive behavior were criticized for their bad influence on children (Wertham 1954). But it wasn't until TV came along that so many violent visual cues were viewed by so many pairs of eyes! As early as 1954, researchers at Yale University found that children's dramatic programs were among the most violent on the air. Concern began to escalate from that point.

Many persons who produce TV programs, however, point to one study that seemed to conclude that violence on TV doesn't matter. Take a close look at it.

The study, done in 1958, focused on the impact of a TV detective series on children. The authors of the study concluded,

> Television is unlikely to cause aggressive behavior although it could precipitate it in those few children who are emotionally disturbed. On the other hand, there was little support for the view that programs of violence are beneficial; we found that they aroused aggression as often as they discharged it.

The study concluded, in effect, that even if viewing violence doesn't harm the average, well-adjusted child, we certainly can't say that it does him any good. Furthermore, TV violence doesn't have a uniform effect on all children.

Many TV producers have extended the study's meaning to conclude that TV violence has *no* impact. That is not at all the intent, tone, or conclusion of the study.

Researchers will never say that one factor *causes* a specific result. They simply do not draw that conclusion. They say that one factor seems to correlate highly with a specific result. They deal with probability.

As Alberta Siegel states,

> Television time is sold to sponsors on the conviction that although an Ajax ad will not guarantee that the viewer will buy the product, it raises the probability that he will. Social scientists could simply make the same claim for filmed or televised violence, whether fictitious or real. Viewing the carnage does not guarantee that the viewer will go forth and do likewise, but it raises the probability that he will.(76:85)

Based on the thousands of studies conducted about TV violence and children, we can reach several specific conclusions about the lessons of violence being taught to our children by The Box.

Children Can Learn Violence from Watching TV

The most famous modeling studies have been done by psychologists Bandura and Walters, who conducted experiments with children in the early 1960s. They exposed nursery-school children to aggressive models to determine if they could find a teaching effect and a motivating effect. On a TV set they showed the children films of models playing aggressively with a Bobo doll as the narrator added such words as *pow, boom, sockeroo.*

One group of children saw only that sequence of actions, but children in two other groups saw additional sequences. One saw the model punished for his acts against the doll; the other saw the model rewarded for his acts. Then the children were taken into a large playroom filled with toys, including a plastic Bobo doll.

Children who had seen the aggressor rewarded for his behavior showed quite a bit of aggressive behavior toward the doll, but those who had seen the model punished, or who had seen no consequences, displayed far fewer aggressive acts against the Bobo doll.

The researchers then offered to reward the children if they could reproduce the model's behavior with the doll. A high percentage of children, including those who had seen the model punished, could reproduce virtually all the model's actions (words and behavior).

This study revealed that children can learn messages from TV and reproduce them. It also revealed that children are less likely to reproduce spontaneously the behavior if they have seen the behavior punished.

A series of take-off studies followed and social-learning-theory researchers made the following conclusions:

- Children could learn as much if the person inflicting pain on the Bobo doll was a cartoon-like figure. Seventy-nine percent of the children who saw the cartoon version exhibited imitative behavior, compared to 88 percent in the other versions.

- Children could still tell how to reproduce an aggressive act up to six to eight months after they had seen the aggressive act on film.

- Children could imitate aggressive acts even when the Bobo doll became a human adult dressed as a clown. Children would mirror aggressive acts even when they knew that harm and pain were being caused and that the enemy was not an unfeeling doll.

The conclusion could readily be drawn that children mimic not only violence but also specific violent behaviors and forms of aggression.

People Who Watch a Lot of Violent TV Behave More Aggressively

One of the best series of studies focusing on TV's impact on children was that conducted by the Television and Social Behavior Program of the U.S. National Institute of Health. Steuer, Applefield, and Smith (1971) conducted one of the studies. The researchers matched pairs of boys and girls on the basis of the amount of time they watched TV at home. Then they established the degree to which the children, in normal play, displayed acts of aggression against one another (such as hitting, kicking, choking, etc.).

Next, the researchers had one child in the pair watch an aggressive TV program on eleven different days. The other child in the pair watched a nonaggressive program. The children were then observed again for acts of aggression.

The viewers of aggression and the viewers of nonaggression had remarkably different behavior patterns at the end of the eleven viewing periods; the viewers of aggression were far more aggressive against their mates. In some cases, the children showed an increase of 200 percent to 300 percent in their aggressiveness!

More than fifty studies have been conducted along similar lines, and all have reached the same conclusion: *the amount of violence a child sees is correlated significantly with the amount of aggression a child displays.*

The most extensive study ever done on TV violence was that conducted by Rowell Huesmann and Leonard Eron. They surveyed the viewing habits of the entire third-grade class in one New York county, and then took a second look at that class when the students reached the age of thirty.

Of those with criminal records, the ones who had watched more TV violence as children were convicted as adults of crimes significantly more violent than others of their peers. The study also found that girls who had watched more TV violence than their peers tended to punish their children more harshly.

Since 1982, TV violence has increased 780 percent. During that same period, schoolteachers report a nearly 800 percent increase in aggressive acts on playgrounds. These are the same children who are watching violent acts on TV at a rate of as many as eighty per half hour, and who spend up to one-third of their waking hours in front of a TV set. We have no doubt that children are stimulated to act more aggressively as a result of what they see on TV.

Then what keeps all children from becoming criminals?

Most children have mitigating circumstances. They have parents who say no to aggression. They have teachers and school administrators who say no to violence. They have someone who punishes their acts of aggression.

The main problem occurs when children don't have parents who punish aggression, or parents are absent when aggression occurs, or children live in an environment in which aggression is rewarded.

TV Affects People in Different Ways

When is aggressiveness most likely to be exhibited?

First, aggressiveness happens when a villain is rewarded for his actions or fails to be punished or criticized (Bandura 1965; Bandura, Ross, and Ross 1964; Rosekrans and Hartup 1967; Lefcourt, Barnes, Parke, and Schwart 1966).

Failure to be punished may also be interpreted as having had no consequences. TV violence generally comes packaged with no consequences.

The villains of Saturday morning, while thoroughly trounced in each episode, rise up to fight another day. They are never ultimately defeated.

The most frequent violent act depicted is the blow to the head with a blunt instrument. Generally the character is rendered unconscious for a short while, then awakens to continue the chase.

Unfortunately, just about any child can carry out this act of aggression. But the real-life consequences of being hit in this manner are much more severe than those portrayed. A victim may have temporary or permanent loss of motor abilities; the inability to speak or understand speech; convulsions; dizziness; and chronic headaches; and emotional problems ranging from irritability to paranoia. When do we ever see such things on TV?

Again, we must bear in mind that to an adult, violence may have entertainment value. To a child, it's all education.

To an adult, a violent program may deliver an implicit message that crime doesn't pay. The child, however, may see the violence of the crime and the criminal's glamorous lifestyle and the criminal's subsequent downfall and may fail to see any relationship whatsoever between the crime and the punishment!

This conclusion is all the more exaggerated, of course, if the child cannot truly differentiate the good guys from the bad guys in a program. On Saturday morning, good guys and bad guys often operate with the same methods. The rewards go to the bad guys as often and as generously as they go to the good guys. Someone simply loses a little power or turf, and that only momentarily.

As a whole, violent acts on children's programs are virtually pain free. People fall from bullet or laser-gun wounds and die instantly. Others have time for a seemingly pain-free poetic farewell statement before slumping over into stillness. Some victims are vaporized so that they are not even seen as wounded!

We should perhaps note that in the "Voltron" and "Transformers" animated programs, some characters were actually killed. The killing was allowed under the thinking that they were robots; therefore, killing them was okay.

Second, aggressiveness is most likely to be exhibited when the violence is depicted in some way as justified (Berkowitz and Rawlings 1963; Meyer 1972).

In virtually every act of aggression displayed on Saturday mornings, the underlying motive seems to be that those who exhibit aggression have the right to do so, at least from their own perspectives. Thus, the villains of Saturday morning have a right to act like villains. The good guys have the right to use aggression against the villains. And so forth and so on until everyone has a right to act as he or she chooses with no higher consequences imposed by law.

Third, an act of aggression is most likely to occur when the villain is most like the person watching the show (Berkowitz and Green 1966; Rosekrans 1967).

The amount of violent detail shown does not, on its own, prescribe the level of fear the viewer experiences or the subsequent
aggressive behavior. The viewer's capacity to empathize with the
victims of violence or the perpetrators of violence results in either
fear or aggressive behavior.

Violence is far more acceptable to us when we have no empathy
with its victims. For example, violence levied against a family member shocks us far more deeply than a report of violence against a
stranger. Even more so, because human prejudices run deeply, we
rarely feel shock over violence inflicted on victims who are alien to
us—those of another race or nation, those we don't understand, or
those we dislike. We tend to feel that violence occurs to some people
because they have asked for it.

Many people point to the cathartic value of violence. They say
people mentally rehearse violence out of their systems so they will
not actually display violent behavior in real life. Any cathartic value
of violence, however, is present only when the victims of violence
are characters with whom we feel a strong identification, or who are
obviously innocent creatures. In cartoons on Saturday mornings, the
bad guys are rarely portrayed as innocent, and rarely can a child
identify with them.

Fourth, aggressive behavior is more likely to occur if the violence
is perceived to cause serious injury (Berkowitz and Alioto 1973;
Green and Stonner 1972).

It may be helpful at this point to define *violence.* One of the most
common definitions is that of Gerbner, a major researcher in the area
of TV and aggression: "The overt expression of physical force
against others or self, or the compelling of action against one's will
on pain of being hurt or killed."

We might also ask, What exactly is the action that makes an action cartoon? Very often it is physical action that results in violence
—karate chops, eye gouges, kicks to the kidneys and groin area, and
other hand-to-hand boxing or wrestling moves. These acts are generally, in the context of Saturday morning, intended to express
physical force, and they occur against one's will, causing pain or
death.

Is it violence to portray an accidental fall down the stairs? Is violence a humorous insult that may be considered emotional battering

or emotional abuse? Is violence an earthquake or other act of God? Is it a fistfight? A war between nations? Probably most of the above, to one degree or other, could be considered violence because all involve the infliction of pain and suffering on human beings.

Fifth, aggressive behavior is more likely to occur when the violence is seen as part of highly exciting content (Tannenbaum and Zillmann 1975; Zillmann 1971).

Close-up shots, camera angles, and sophisticated film editing techniques can make violence even more graphic and larger than life. A steady undercurrent of music and sound effects also adds to the horror of many violent scenes. These techniques amplify fear in small children. Small children simply cannot comprehend that in real life, music rarely underscores an about-to-be-committed murder. The violent acts are often portrayed using these techniques so that the violent action becomes something of a climax. It's an end result that brings with it a release of tension, and in that the act becomes a good thing because it relaxes the tone of the movie and the muscles of the viewer! It also releases the anxiety or suspense that has been built up in the viewer's mind. In the real world, a child is more likely to exhibit aggressive behavior and to commit an act of violence to experience that same release of pent-up emotions.

Sixth, aggressive behavior is more likely to occur when the child is already predisposed to be aggressive.

A study done in England concluded that children predisposed to aggression were those who had developed few interests of their own, came from low-income families, and had unsatisfactory human relationships. (We can't help wondering if those same children watched a great deal of TV as preschoolers and failed to develop other interests.)

In many studies, boys are found to be more naturally aggressive than girls. For example, an early study by Bandura compared the aggression scores of boys and girls when they viewed behavior by real-life characters, filmed characters, and a cartoon cat. The study indicated that boys are generally twice as aggressive as girls by the time they reach school age. Many of today's cartoons are aimed at boys, apparently only further exacerbating their aggressive tendencies.

Aggression, at a basic level, is an instinct. Certain cues from the environment can elicit fear, which gives rise to a flight-or-fight mechanism in most of us. In the face of danger, we'll choose either to stand our ground or to run away. This type of aggressive behavior, however, is triggered from the outside.

Another type of aggression seems to stem from within. Persons with inside aggressive tendencies are likely to act aggressively in most situations. This type of aggression is learned behavior.

A child can observe aggression and learn it in several ways. He can see it enacted in the home. He can experience it as it is manifested against himself, often to the point of abuse. He can also see it on TV. It doesn't seem to make much difference which comes first.

The most aggressive children tend to live in aggressive homes and watch a great deal of aggression on The Box. TV violence can give rise to aggressive acts, which are reinforced for the child by the aggression experienced in everyday life. Or the aggression a child witnesses and receives in everyday life may be reinforced by what he sees on TV. Either way, a cycle is created that is difficult to break.

McCarthy and associates conducted a five-year study involving 732 children in which they concluded that a child's aggression—exhibited in the form of fights with parents, fights with peers, or general delinquency—was correlated positively with the watching of TV violence. The more violence watched, the higher the levels of aggression. They also determined that children without desirable life events tended to watch more TV.

Why Not Denounce Violence on TV?

Although many varied and prominent groups have denounced TV violence, it continues as if no statements were ever made against it.

In 1968, the National Commission on the Causes and Prevention of Violence stated,

> We believe it is reasonable to conclude that a constant diet of violent behavior on television has an adverse effect on human character and attitudes. Violence on television encourages violent forms of behavior, and fosters moral and social values about violence in daily life which are unacceptable in a civilized society. . . . It is a matter of grave concern that at a time when the values and the influence of traditional

institutions such as family, church, and school are in question, television is emphasizing violent, antisocial styles of life.

The December 1975 *Journal of the American Medical Association* featured an article by Dr. Michael Rothenberg, a noted Seattle pediatrician, who wrote about TV violence and called for "a major, organized cry of protest from the medical profession in relation to what, in political terms, I consider a national scandal" (p. 1043).

In response to this article, congressional interest was aroused as the doctors, major contributors to campaigns and the backers of a powerful Washington lobby, exerted their influence. The AMA House of Delegates resolved that it would:

- declare its recognition of the fact that TV violence is a risk factor threatening the health and welfare of young Americans, indeed, our future society.
- commit itself to remedial action in concert with industry, government and other interested parties.
- encourage all physicians, their families and their patients to actively oppose TV programs containing violence, as well as products and/or services sponsoring such programs. (American Medical Association Policy 1976)

The national PTA organization launched a similar campaign against TV violence in 1976. Together, the AMA and PTA efforts influenced TV programmers. The level of violence on programs aired in 1977 dropped significantly.

But the decrease didn't hold.

In the late 1960s, Professor George Gerbner at the University of Pennsylvania's Graduate School of Communication developed something he called a violence index to tally body counts and kill ratios of TV programs. Senator Pastore, chairman of the Subcommittee on Communications of the Senate Commerce Committee, thought the violence index should be published to alert the nation to the amount of violent imagery in programs made available over public airwaves. The idea never got off the ground. The networks and the National Association of Broadcasters claimed vehemently that there was no conclusive evidence that violent TV shows resulted in violent antisocial behavior. Some even claimed, and continue to claim, that it is cathartic for society to watch violence.

Jesse Steinfeld's "TV Violence IS Harmful" appeared in the May 1973 issue of *Reader's Digest,* and he concluded, "We can no longer tolerate the present high level of televised violence that is put before children in American homes" (p. 38).

But we continue to tolerate violence on TV. Furthermore, cartoon programming has increased significantly in its rate of violence per program over the past decade.

The Arguments for Violence

A number of arguments have been made in favor of TV violence or in dismissal of its effects.

Some people point to the moral conclusions that often appear on violent TV programs denouncing violence or drawing a positive benefit. On "G.I. Joe," for example, often a thirty-second conclusion, of sorts, provides a lesson about being kind to animals or about using safety devices. This disclaimer comes after twenty-two minutes of violent education, however.

Some people point out that aggressive behavior and competition are parts of our society. Aggression in our culture, unfortunately, is still merged with the idea of competitiveness and with energetic assertiveness in the minds of many people. Few role models on Saturday morning tell a child that it's okay to compete, but that competition doesn't need to turn into a power play. Virtually no messages say that competition is possible without aggressive behavior.

Assertiveness can be exercised through dialogue and discussion or by ignoring the taunts of an enemy. You will not learn those lessons, however, by watching TV on Saturday morning.

Some people argue that violence is a part of human nature and that one must teach a child about violence to help the child cope with it. That argument has three fallacies.

In the first place, teaching a child *about* violence is different from teaching a child violence. We can teach a child about the atomic bomb by telling him what it is made of, the general principles of its operation, and so on. We do not teach children about the atomic bomb by giving them one. We can also teach our children about violence without giving them a constant dose of it.

In the second place, unless one teaches about violence, a child really has no coping skills for violence experienced in real life. The only alternative shown is that of more violence. To give a child coping skills means to provide alternatives to aggression and violent responses. A child must also be taught the rudiments of justice.

Finally, no evidence substantiates that showing a steady stream of violent images to children helps them cope with life. The opposite seems to be better supported. Children respond to violence by perceiving life as more anxiety ridden and the world as a more fearful place. In the end, the promulgation of fear may be the foremost detrimental aspect of violence on TV.

Fear

Fear has two main types. One is self-preserving and rooted in reality. The other is self-destructive and rooted in illusion.

Of one thing we can be fairly certain: when children see violence on TV that is more intense than what they experience in the real world, they get a distorted perception of the world. They tend to believe the TV version of the state of the world more than what they experience.

A 1977 study at Temple University reported that children between seven and eleven years of age who were heavy TV viewers were more likely to be scared more often than those who were light TV viewers. The heavy viewers were fearful of the world at large, frightened that someone bad would come into their homes, and afraid that when they went outside someone would hurt them.

In a study by Gerbner, heavy TV viewers in both New York City and New Jersey—a more rural and small-town population—were surveyed to determine their opinions about the world and violence. Most of the New Jersey students, about 80 percent, felt it was dangerous to walk alone in a city at night—any city!

Girls had a more fearful outlook than boys on their worlds both in New York City and in New Jersey. Younger students were more fearful than older ones. Heavy TV viewers had higher levels of mistrust for others and expressed more often the belief that people were selfish.

What happens to a child's mood when he sees violence? Biblow, in a 1973 study, found that children's moods often shifted from anger to shame to sadness as they watched an aggressive film. When they watched a nonaggressive film, their moods shifted from anger to elation.

Fantasy helps create mood changes. Children who are accustomed to fantasy respond to a fantasy situation with a wide range of moods, the same as if the situation were real.

The possibility is very real that children's responses to TV violence may well be depression about life.

Whether cartoons and toys provoke actual acts of aggression may not be the most significant point; at least, it may not be the only point. Children are harmed when their feelings of anger and frustration are increased as a result of their watching TV violence.

Dr. Glenn Sparks, Purdue University, was quoted in an interview as saying,

> Between the ages of seven and eleven, children frequently mention that violent TV scenes frighten and upset them. Children this age realize these scenes could really happen—and happen to them. They're not ready to cope with this yet. The availability of scary scenes has risen dramatically with the proliferation of cable TV and VCR's. Many children who saw *Friday the 13th* or *Halloween* are afraid robbers will come and chop them up.

Fear generally is expressed when a person, including a child, doesn't feel he or she has any control over a situation or any power to escape a situation.

What about Desensitization?

Given the sheer amount of time a child is exposed to TV violence, how can a child not become jaded, desensitized, and inured to its impact, not only on TV but also in real life?

An eleven-year-old said, "You see so much violence that it's meaningless. If I saw someone really get killed, it wouldn't be a big deal. I guess I'm turning into a hard rock."

That boy wasn't born a hard rock. He was taught to be one. He was trained to be one.

What happens to a child physiologically when he sees violence? What takes place in her body?

In one study, researchers measured the heart rates of children who viewed three TV episodes, one of dramatic violence with actors, another with cartoon violence, and a third with a neutral program. The heart rates of the children decreased during both violent episodes, whether animated or dramatic. The heart rates of younger subjects decreased more than those of older subjects (Surbeck 1973). In other words, the children seemed to shut down during violence, showing a physiological reaction and a common defense mechanism even though no changes may have been visible.

In yet another study, researchers looked at the pulse amplitude (range) of children. They found that children who were heavy TV viewers had less change in their pulse amplitudes than those who were light viewers when violent programs were shown to them.

Researchers call these results desensitization. Desensitization is a method of treatment that is widely used, with great success, to cure neurotic patients of anxieties, phobias, obsessive-compulsive neuroses, and other emotional disorders. Usually the feelings the patients hold are considered too strong or too long lasting for the patients to be willing to have them any longer, and the patients generally seek a therapist who can help.

What happens when desensitization is used as a method of treatment? The process is not unlike what happens to children as they watch TV violence!

The goal of the therapist is to help the person show literally no reaction when she is faced with an object she fears.

Fear and anxiety involve tension. Muscles tense up as part of the neurotic response. Relaxation, therefore, which is the opposite of anxiety both physiologically and psychologically, is a prime method of treatment.

In normal therapy conditions, a patient is often taught certain relaxation techniques. Counter-conditioning treatment then begins. The feared object is gradually introduced to the patient, who uses his newly learned relaxation techniques to alleviate his normal anxiety response.

Many times these techniques are accompanied by emotional re-education. Psychodrama, sociodrama, and role-playing exercises are used. These activities provide opportunities for rehearsal and repetition, allowing new associations to entrench themselves more securely.

But imaginal desensitization erodes many of a person's past relationships to symbols, images, and events.

The parallels to TV are immense.

Relaxation is coupled with violence. The release of anxiety at dramatic moments through the move to commercial breaks virtually conditions a relaxation response to violent acts. The constant repetition allows the viewer to watch more and more violence, with less and less reaction. Ultimately, the TV experience itself becomes a pleasant alternative to everyday violence and tension, so that one would rather watch murders than deal with the family budget.

Erma Bombeck once wrote an angry letter to television networks in which she said:

> During a single evening I saw twelve people shot, two tortured, one dumped into a swimming pool, two cars explode, a rape, and a man who crawled two blocks with a knife in his stomach. Do you know something? I didn't feel anger or shock or horror or excitement or repugnance. The truth is I didn't feel. Through repeated assaults of one violent act after another, you have taken from me something I valued —something that contributed to my compassion and caring—the instinct to feel.

Many people enjoy sentimental movies. These adults often are amazed to find that when they begin to show emotion, children turn around to watch them rather than the TV. The children have seen so many hours of televised emotion that it just doesn't mean anything anymore. Several studies have reached the conclusion that children who are heavy TV viewers actually reach the state where violence has no meaning in reality for them.

In a 1974 study, Drabman and Thomas found that exposure to TV violence increased a child's tolerance for real-life aggression. The children who saw programs with aggression were much slower in getting adult help when fights broke out among children on the playground.

The researchers concluded in a follow-up study in 1976 that children who are exposed to a great deal of fictional violence on TV come to believe that "aggression is a way of American life and therefore not to be taken seriously." Furthermore, because the violence on TV is more vicious than what the children experience on the school playground or in their neighborhoods, the everyday brand of violence seems mild and not worthy of intervention.

Charles E. Silberman tells in his book *Criminal Violence, Criminal Justice* about two boys, twelve and thirteen years old, who set fire to a cat and then murdered a derelict as he slept by dousing him with lighter fluid and setting him afire. Silberman wrote,

> The absence of affect [in the boys] is the most frightening aspect of all. In the past, juveniles who exploded into violence tended to feel considerable guilt or remorse afterward; the new criminals have been so brutalized in their upbringing that they seem incapable of viewing victims as fellow human beings, or of realizing that they have killed another person.

Conflict Resolution

By limiting a viewer's emotional response to issues and actions that should evoke response, television's conditioning effect for violence also tends to limit the avenues by which young viewers learn how to resolve conflicts.

With the ceaseless repetition of a message that conflict may be resolved by aggression, and even that conflict is usually resolved by aggressive acts, children learn that violence is a way, and perhaps even the preferred way, of solving problems. They come to expect aggression as a part of problem solving.

This expectation of violence and passivity in the face of it has far greater implications for society than do persons who inflict violence.

How can we say that? Because those who inflict violence are usually punished, in real life. They face consequences.

But What About . . .

When I discuss violence with parents in seminars across the nation, I repeatedly encounter a series of *But what about*'s:

But what about fairy tales? Aren't they violent? The difference between fairy-tale violence and TV cartoon violence is extreme.

Violence in classical literature is usually one aspect of an overall plot or characterization. One doesn't encounter violence for violence's sake. Also, violence is considered aberrant behavior. Violent acts are considered tragedies. Violence is nearly always couched in terms of a moral or emotional struggle and the result of inner turmoil and interpersonal conflict.

These factors are missing in violent cartoons.

The violence in fairy tales is aimed in a different direction than that of cartoons. Fairy-tale writers often include violence to make the point that violence is the consequence of wayward behavior by otherwise good people. The message is: if you obey your parents and never run away from home, you won't encounter a wicked witch in the dark forest who will bake you in her oven. Fairy tales also frequently couch acts of violence against bad guys as acts of self-defense. For example, the three little pigs built a fire in their fireplace as an act of self-defense against the big bad wolf.

In today's cartoons, violence is rarely the result of an act of self-defense, and it is rarely the consequence of wayward behavior by otherwise good people. The villains generally are drawn as villains from the outset; they are seemingly born to be bad. Often, both parties seem out to conquer a third and more neutral target.

"But people like to watch violence," others say. Most broadcasters tend to think that nothing is wrong with violence in cartoons and that violence is truly enjoyed by the public, including children. Broadcasters view violence as action and fantasy and, in that, good TV.

What does the public think? The general prevailing view of society is that violence is unwholesome, undesirable, and unhealthy, in that it causes injury and hurt both to individual people and to society as a whole. Violence is a reminder of the dark side in all of us that can all too easily overwhelm those who are fragile in their personalities, as well as swamp relationships that might also be called fragile. We intuitively shy away from violence; yet we watch it.

Why? In part, because violence is often coupled with suspense, and human beings like suspense. Suspense is rooted in the unknown and in surprise. And most human beings are curious creatures who enjoy surprises. Most of us are even willing to risk a bad surprise only because most of the surprises we experience are good or pleasurable at some level.

We also like to see good guys win over bad guys, and occasionally the victory requires violence. We like to see human beings overcome the violence of nature. Finally, some violence is actually couched in humor and wit. We suffer the violence to see the jokester at work, whether his name is James Bond or Donald Duck.

On Saturday morning, however, violence is rarely coupled with suspense; it is coupled with scheming.

Saturday morning violence is rarely couched in terms of man against beast. More often than not, beasts are friends, or the battle is among beasts.

Dinerd and DeFour studied eleven action-adventure programs over an entire viewing season (1978) and found no relationship between harsh violence and ratings. They also presented two versions of a program called "Police Woman" to subjects and found no greater preference for the version with harsh violence.

Why, then, are violent programs repeatedly offered on TV?

Programs with violent incidents increase and decrease in quantity according to the perception by those in the TV business of their popularity. The growth of violence actually has little to do with the appetite for violence among viewers.

Indeed, "The Cosby Show," "Roseanne," "Cheers," and "Murphy Brown" were the most consistently rated top shows aired during prime-time hours in 1989. None of them were violent.

It seems far more likely to us that viewers respond most favorably to the depth, wit, and interaction of characters and to the degree to which those characters elicit empathy or a heartwarming tug on the part of the viewer.

Thus, if the viewer responds favorably to Angie Dickinson as the lead character on "Police Woman" and likes her relationship with the other characters, she will rate the program high—no matter how much violence is included. If the character or star had been a dud, the program probably would have declined in popularity, without regard to the violence.

Producers seem to fail to understand that when a program devotes more time to violent action, it devotes less time to characterizations. Viewers want to know the characters, to learn from them, to like them and feel kinship with them. And the more time a character spends in defensive or offensive action, the less time she has for exploring her feelings.

Clark and Blankenburg took a look in 1972 at a sixteen-year period in TV history and specifically at the violent nature of TV programs. They found that violence tended to peak every four years, and that the growth and decline of violence correlated positively with the average ratings for violent programs the year before.

A violent TV season tended to spawn a more-violent TV season, until the programming reached the point that the viewing public cried uncle and turned its dial to programs with more gentle themes, stronger characterizations, and more fully developed relationships among characters. The violence chokes out the characters; the violence grows but the characterizations don't. And after the peak comes the time when viewers again search for a character they can know and like.

Most people assume that cartoons are saturated with violence because children want to see violence. That isn't the case at all.

Violence fills Saturday morning programs because of the broadcasters' choices and, to some degree, their lack of creativity. Children like action and motion, and broadcasters choose violence as a cheap and uncreative way to provide action and motion.

Children are more interested in situation comedies or educational programs. In one study, first graders rated their two favorite programs as "My Favorite Martian" and "I Love Lucy." In another study, preschoolers strongly preferred "Sesame Street" to violent cartoons. Children also like something that makes them laugh, that helps them learn something they didn't know before, and that can be grasped quickly and easily.

Program creators seem to have interpreted these preferences as being for slapstick humor, although children will laugh at far more than that; an emphasis on the unusual; and simple messages rooted in fast action. Our contention is that children are as happy with Mister Rogers as they are with He-Man. And Fred Rogers doesn't blow people away.

Children never clamored for crime and horror TV. Their appetite for violence was cultivated—by adults who have fed them violence from children's first encounters with The Box.

Persons who claim that children like violence and want violence often base that opinion on their belief that children are naturally aggressive. This appears to be true. Children are aggressive, especially small children. But that isn't the whole story.

Studies indicate that older children seem to have learned hostility as a motive for their aggressive acts. They are likely to strike out with the intent of harming someone else. Children may be born aggressive, but they are not born mean. Meanness is not a natural trait; it is learned. Saturday morning's violent cartoons only help in that educational process toward meanness.

The Big Picture

We would be remiss if we didn't also look at some of the larger social patterns. Of course, at the outset we make no claims that cartoons, cartoons plus toy play, or television as a whole is solely responsible for triggering these patterns, or even that the factors are directly correlated. Nevertheless, let's consider the big picture for a moment.

The present generation is

- killing itself at a rate that reflects a 300 percent increase over the previous generation, and the murder rate of black youths aged fourteen to twenty-four in the U.S. is four times greater than that of any other industrialized nation on earth

- experiencing rape of women at a rate that reflects a 500 percent increase over the previous generation

- assaulting one another at a rate that is 600 percent more often, per capita, than the previous generation

Consider, too, the instances of child abuse. The number of children under the age of five who are killed each year by a parent is greater than the number of those who die from disease. An estimated one million children are beaten, burned, thrown, kicked, or battered each year. Exact figures are unknown since not all cases are reported to officials. These statistics are related to the first generation of parents who were raised on TV when they were children.

A study of one hundred juvenile offenders was commissioned by the ABC network. Researchers found that at least twenty-five of the offenders had copied criminal techniques from TV (71:78).

A Ray of Good News

The good news is that children can learn something else besides violence.

Kniveton concluded in his 1974 study that the viewing of violence can be lessened if the child has other intellectual stimulation besides TV. Children with few interests are more susceptible to imitating TV models.

Television can also be used to teach coping skills to children. For example, Bandura and Menlove demonstrated in their study (1968) that a child's fear of dogs can be greatly reduced by his watching programs in which children and dogs play together. Children have also learned not to fear their dentists by watching a program showing a pleasant visit to a dentist's office (Hill, Liebert, and Mott 1968). Even psychotherapists have found that patients who watch TV programs showing appropriate behavior can learn that behavior and display it in their lives (Alger and Hogan 1967, 1969).

Prosocial programs do work. They do teach.

Prosocial programs are generally perceived to be those that include these behaviors:

- spontaneously giving or loaning something, providing assistance to help another, working together
- choosing an alternative behavior to aggression in frustrating situations
- apologizing and admitting a mistake
- not taking a smaller reward to qualify for a larger reward later, showing persistence and delay of gratification
- explaining feelings rather than acting on them
- resisting a temptation to hurt someone
- verbalizing sympathy or concern for others and their problems

Collins and Getz reported in a 1976 study that children from fourth through tenth grades were more helpful to their peers after they saw an action-adventure program that had constructive, cooperative problem solving than were children who saw a neutral program or an aggressive one.

Programs that portray prosocial messages teach those messages, and children learn them. Programs that portray aggression and violence teach those messages, and children learn them.

Which curriculum do we want to provide for our children?

So What's a Parent to Do?

Watch your child. Look for acts of aggression, increased agitation and fits of temper, and increased lack of caring about others, especially those who are sick or in pain. Be alert to the occurrence of nightmares. Watch for increased or new patterns of bed-wetting. Look for new instances in which the child appears to be afraid.

Those are all immediate and urgent cues for you to take charge of your child's TV viewing with an iron hand. Turn off The Box. Talk to your child about what makes her afraid. Try to isolate whether a specific instance of TV viewing caused the behavior, and attempt to talk through it with your child.

Use this quick five-count way to evaluate the violent content of a cartoon before you let your child watch it regularly:

1. Count the number of different weapons in the cartoon and try to keep track of the number of times each is used. If more than three are used, or one is used more than three times, turn it off.

2. Count the number of people killed. If anyone is killed, turn it off.

3. Count the number of unprovoked attacks (whether the character is good or bad). If there are any, turn it off.

4. How do the good characters resolve conflict? Do they use the same methods as the bad guys? If so, turn it off.

5. Do the good guys break laws? If so, turn it off.

As a general rule, and especially one to share with baby-sitters, limit your child's TV viewing to programs that you know have a prosocial message. It's best to eliminate programs containing violence for children under five.

Chapter Six

The World on The Box

There is nothing more political than the opportunities a social system holds out to its members, permitting and encouraging them to live in imagination the lives of others whose fates in the social system are otherwise. Literature and art, drama and music, song and story, ballads and rhymes and chants, tales and play and games, myth and history help us do this.

When they are authentic, they help us see and feel the many human conditions that make up the human condition, and thus to realize our own. When they are inauthentic, they muddle thought, drop a veil between us and our fellow human beings, disguise our own social realities.

—Educator Rose K. Golden

Television is a false mirror. It reflects what appears to be reality, but it does *not* reflect the real world.

The violence portrayed on TV is pseudorealism. The continuity of experience is missing. Children rarely see a full display of the consequences of violence: jail, trials, expenses, grief and mourning; the effects on the lives of the victims; or the impact on the family, neighborhood, or society at large. Little is explained about why a person becomes violent in the first place, or why he becomes a villain. Violence on TV isn't grounded in a social context or rooted in a social ethic.

In executing the law, animated figures rarely provide for constitutional protection of private citizens. Animated gangs generally operate according to vigilante codes of behavior.

Criminals rarely are held personally responsible for their crimes. Blame is nearly always placed on society for denying the criminal certain freedoms or privileges, for ignoring the criminal's pent-up anger, or for failing the criminal in some way.

Even the rare cases in which villains are punished may not offset the impact of their behavior since most villains receive immediate rewards, and immediate rewards to children are far more influential than delayed punishment in regulating behavior. Never mind that the criminal goes to jail. He gets to drive the shiny car and date the beautiful girls and live in the fancy mansion for awhile first.

What is the perceived motivation for violence or criminal acts on TV? Many acts of crime or aggression seem to be grounded in the criminal's inability to participate in the so-called good life enjoyed by a certain segment of the community in which he lives. Criminals seem to be people who feel cheated, demoralized, or thwarted in their personal attempts to succeed. It seems ironic that characters with such motives are presented on TV, the medium that has done the most to create the very illusion of a good life for so many.

What exactly is the world portrayed on Saturday morning and elsewhere?

First, it is a world with skewed demographics.

George Gerner and Larry Gross summarized a series of studies done in the late 1970s to come up with this startling set of facts:

In one week, the typical prime-time viewer watching a single network station is likely to encounter 300 dramatic characters with speaking roles. This does not include those on game shows, in the news, in documentaries, and on commercials.

- Of those 300 dramatic characters, 217 will be male, about 80 will be female, and a handful will be animals, robots, or other entities not clearly definable as male or female.

- Of the 300 characters, 262 will be white, 35 will be of other races, and 3 will be someone whose race is hard to tell.

During the weekend and daytime children's viewing hours, the child will encounter 137 dramatic characters with the same gender and race ratios as those listed above.

- On the world of TV, 75 percent of the characters are American and are between 30 and 60 years old; children and the elderly are neglected. In reality, the U.S. has less than 5 percent of the world's population, and only 33 percent of its population is between 30 and 60.

- On TV, 75 percent of the characters are male. In the real world, only about 49.5 percent of the U.S. population is male.

This trend is even more exaggerated in children's TV. Only one of the "Dino-Riders" is a woman (Serena), all the original "Smurfs" were males (the only female in the group being a male who has undergone a sex transformation), and all of the "Teenage Mutant Ninja Turtles" are males. "G.I. Joe" and virtually all the programs linked to action-figure toy series are exclusively or all-but-one-male programs.

And what about the folks doing the selling on commercials that air during children's viewing hours?

Seven out of ten are male, including male action figures. And 97 percent are white.

Second, one will find on TV stereotypic beliefs about social roles for men and women.

Fureh and McGhee reported a study in 1975 in which they looked at whether heavy TV viewers would have more stereotypic beliefs than light viewers. Among their stereotypes were that girls should play with dolls, dishes, and dresses, while boys should play with trucks, guns, and tools. They found significant evidence that both boys and girls in kindergarten, second, fourth, and sixth grades identified more with the sex-stereotyped roles associated with their gender if they were heavy viewers than if they were light viewers.

Even on "Sesame Street," Big Bird has been told he is a "boy bird and will have to help with men's work, important work, heavy work" and that he "should get a girl bird to help Susan with her work of flower arranging" (Gardner 1970).

Women shown on TV are often exaggerated. Consider "She-Ra—Princess of Power," introduced by Filmation as a female counterpart to "He-Man and Masters of the Universe." Said the vice president of the company that produces the show, "We always wanted to do a series with resourceful women in the lead, women who did not need men to save them." But what kind of a woman role model is She-Ra? She has special magic powers and healing powers.

Diana Foutz compared the attractiveness of three different dolls as role models to young boys and girls: She-Ra, Barbie, Mrs. Heart. She interviewed four- to six-year-olds about which doll they would want as a mentor, friend, and mother. Boys were given the option of choosing a girlfriend rather than a mentor.

Foutz found that the girls felt strongly that Mrs. Heart would make the best mother and friend, but that She-Ra would be the best mentor. The boys chose She-Ra as a mother, girlfriend, and friend!

Women, more often than men, are the victims of violence. Victims are also minority women more often than white women and older women more often than younger women.

Third, one will find on TV distorted images about jobs and occupations.

A study from radio research can be applied to TV. In the study, children heard two versions of a radio drama about a taxi driver. In one program, the taxi driver got into trouble with another person and became violently aggressive. In the second program, the taxi driver and the other person resolved their difficulty in a nonaggressive manner (Siegel 1958).

The children were then asked to read and report to the researchers how certain newspaper articles might end. One story was about a local taxi driver. Those children who had heard the violent ending to the radio drama gave very different responses from those who had heard the nonviolent ending. They generally included violence in their conclusions. A stereotype had been created for them as the result of a media report.

The military also has been stereotyped. Most military men on TV are cast as stiff and bureaucratic, with few human feelings. Often our own military is pictured as whipping up some type of imaginary threat or blundering through an unnecessary or ill-conceived maneuver. As portrayed on television, the military doesn't seem to have much useful value beyond its own self-preservation.

What about the average businessman? Many are portrayed as con men or criminals. Others are depicted as wealthy, fat, braggadocious entrepreneurs; still others are rigid, mean, right-wing conservative bankers and landlords determined to destroy the weak, poor, and helpless.

What about police officers? TV programs make it appear that virtually all police are involved as investigators of crimes or as those responsible for working on special forces that tackle drug rings, spy rings, or various other rings. Little is shown of the police officer who performs fairly routine duties, or who leads a fairly normal life with a family in a suburban home. And some TV cops have given in to crime's rewards and are shown to be participating in crime.

Fourth, one will find on TV an exaggerated emphasis on beauty. In a study by Tan (1979), teenage girls exposed to a heavy dose of beauty commercials were more likely to believe that being beautiful is an important characteristic and that beauty is necessary for attracting men than were teens who did not see the commercials.

The message of many dolls (such as Barbie) and animated programs is also this: little girls must be prepared for a life of buying clothes, cosmetics, and accessories that will make them irresistible objects to men. This all promotes the idea that life is a look.

The implication of many cartoon programs is that if you're ugly, you must be evil, and if you're beautiful, you must be okay. It will be interesting to see how today's children feel about *The Elephant Man* or *The Hunchback of Notre Dame* someday.

Fifth, one will find on TV a distorted view of other nationalities, cultures, and races.

For many children, TV is the primary source of information about people of other races, ethnic groups, social classes, and cultures. In one study, 40 percent of a group of 300 elementary school students from urban, suburban, and rural areas responded that they had learned from TV most of what they knew about black people in terms of their looks, manner of speaking, and dress (Greenberg 1972).

Foreigners often are portrayed as causing violence, and they are more likely to pay for causing it. Says a noted movie producer,

> The movies and their toy spin-offs are teaching children to think of people of other nationalities as violence-crazed murderers who can only be dealt with by violence. If you're a little kid, you can't lug around an M-16 to protect yourself, so the next best thing is to head for cover. (88:27)

And those comments also apply to TV. Asians, Hispanics, and Indians rarely are seen on TV as heroes.

Television need not promote prejudicial stereotypes. It has been shown to influence positively the attitudes of children toward minorities, foreigners, and people who in general are different from them. Two studies involving preschoolers showed that children responded more favorably to other children who were not like themselves after watching segments of "Sesame Street" or "Mister Rogers" that were devoted to those themes (Collins 1976; Gorn,

Goldberg, and Kanungo 1976). ITT sponsored a series entitled "Big Blue Marble" in the 1970s that presented vignettes about children from all over the world. In a formal study, children showed a positive reaction both to the series and to other children of dissimilar backgrounds.

The prejudices on Saturday morning are glaring. The bad guys rarely are like individuals watching the programs. Many are no longer people at all but creatures that invite destruction.

A major problem can occur when such an image of reality is extended to the real world. Who decides when someone is asking for it? Is violence acceptable if it happens to someone who is not of our own kind? Is violence all right if the person hurt wasn't an innocent human being?

As reported in the *L.A. Parent Magazine* (April 1987), Carole Lieberman, Ph.D., says,

> The idea of what a stranger is can vary from someone you don't know to someone from a different town or country. It's necessary to distinguish between different kinds of strangers. . . . I think it was the fantasy of a lot of children that when the Columbia [space shuttle] blew up it was the creatures from outer space retaliating. If you have aggressive impulses toward someone, and they do something, you may interpret that as aggression toward you when in fact it is not.

The conclusion to be drawn? Children believe the stereotypes that TV feeds them.

Although older children and teens may be able to discount a TV program as just a story, they, too, often describe the roles and role relationships and dialogue as highly realistic. The values and attitudes inherent in those characterizations and conversations are held at face value. They become lessons as to how one should dress, act, talk, and relate to others in various circumstances.

Studies have shown that TV can cause children to change their attitudes about people and activities. Television is an attitude adjuster for children.

The Mainstreaming of Culture

Television provides little in terms of real segmentation of materials that might appeal to audiences of different ages, regions of the country, or ethnic backgrounds. It could, but it rarely does.

Why? One reason may be that only about fifty people write the vast majority of the cartoons seen today. They work for a limited number of production companies. Nearly all of them earn middle- to upper-range salaries. And nearly all of them live in Los Angeles or New York City.

Another reason no doubt relates to dollars. TV producers sell commercial time according to the number of viewers. Segmenting the audience to appeal to specific age, ethnic, or demographic factors cuts the numbers, dilutes the audience, and drives down the price. Thus, the images presented are nearly always going to be those of the mainstream.

What does this do to a culture, specifically to a society rooted in the melting-pot concept that many cultures can coexist peacefully together? It waters it down. Minority groups are always going to see themselves as minorities shaped by the dominant interests of the larger common culture.

Says Rose Goldsen:

Television now holds a virtual monopoly on whatever artistic and symbolic forms have a chance to be widely shared through the society.
. . . It is in this way that television comes to dominate social thought; less because its journalistic efforts provide a data bank of what we take to be the factual truths about government and politics and civic life, and more because its total efforts monopolize the socially shared lines of sight for surveying social reality and making things familiar. (29:285–86)

To a small child, seeing is believing, and seeing is reality. The lines between fantasy and reality are drawn with a thin, faint, and wavy line. Even if children are aware that the TV stories they see are not real life, they are still subject to the influence of a story, and to the influences they feel with their hearts and not their heads. They can cry or shudder at what they see on the screen as much as if they were seeing it in three dimensions on the playground.

Propaganda is based not on reason and truth but on emotion. It tugs at what we fear, what we love, what we hate, what we hold to be valuable. Cartoons and dramatic shows that evoke strong emotions operate on the same principle. They teach, influence, and even brainwash in the same way.

Dr. Dorothy Cohen of Bank Street College of Education in New York City noted:

> All of society is slipping into a greater reliance on the image of the thing rather than the real thing itself. Television is no better or worse than the rest of society, but it is the major instrument by which, at present, we hasten the process of alienation in our young and interfere with the processes of ego strengthening which grow primarily through contact with reality, not images, through participation and interaction with people and things, not through passivity and imitation.

An adult may be capable of distinguishing between real life and TV reality. A child is not. On TV, people are often portrayed as wanting money and happiness for themselves. The person who chooses not to seek money and happiness as a goal is regarded either as suspect or as saintly. In reality, many people volunteer their time and give money to social and political causes. Where, on TV, will a child learn that?

On TV, life never has a dull moment. Every day holds a new mix-up, a new crisis, a new crime to solve, a new mystery. In reality, most of life has little drama. People get up, get dressed, eat breakfast, go to school or work, come home, watch TV, eat dinner, watch more TV, and go to bed. What parent can compete with the life portrayed by TV moms and dads? Compared to winning wars that will determine the fate of the cosmos—as TV kids do—how can playing a game of catch seem exciting to a child?

On TV, nearly everyone lives a life that is clean and neat, well groomed and hygienic. Shabby boardinghouses are painted brightly and have cheery interiors with lots of light. Even the smallest apartment is furnished tastefully, and most apartments have an amazing amount of space. Even farm barns are immaculate, and wooded areas are free of underbrush and bothersome insects and snakes. Reality offers a much different scenario.

The general tone of TV is also rooted in false reality. Whether the program is a sitcom or a police show, it is likely to have the same optimistic worldview: that everything will come out right in the end, that life has infinite potential, and that the anxieties or worries about daily life are minimal. In reality, tragedies do happen, some things fail, and people do make mistakes with terrible consequences.

No society we know of makes the claim that social stratas don't exist, or that any and every person can change social class at will. Except, of course, on the world of TV. Virtually all characters live a middle-class, upper-middle-class, or wealthy lifestyle. They are educated, have jobs, use good grammar, and wear clean clothes. The sad irony is that children from lower socioeconomic classes watch more TV than ones from the higher classes. These very children, who probably have less chance of changing their strata in society, are shown the most visual cues depicting upper-strata living.

Rarely does a child see a character discuss options of behavior, and rule out various ones for various reasons. Yet this is a normal process in life.

Perhaps one of the falsest lessons a child might draw from TV is that nice guys finish last. In reality, nice people are usually the ones promoted.

TV also raises false expectations about an individual's fallibility. For example, the program "Bionic Six" features the Bennet family of six who possess bionic capabilities that allow them to run faster, see farther, and hear better than other folks. They do not die or get sick —ever. And no matter what goes wrong with the human body, it can be fixed.

What Is Acceptable?

Television also presents a highly artificial view of what is acceptable behavior.

Bart, on "The Simpsons" animated series, routinely has to stay after school to write on the blackboard such statements as "I will not call my teacher 'hot cakes.' " While this punishment leaves the impression that Bart is being punished, it also leaves the impression that Bart is funny and that it's somehow cute for a child to address adults with slang words. In one study, more than seven out of ten parents reported that their children regularly imitated TV characters by using slang expressions and accents (Woodrick et al. 1977).

Acceptable human behavior takes on a whole new meaning on "The Super Mario Bros. Super Show!" programs and videos. On one drama segment, a niece of the Brothers threw a party without permission from her uncles. The Brothers decided to plug their ears against the loud music rather than exert disciplinary measures because they didn't want to hurt the teens' feelings. During animated segments of "The Super Mario Bros.," you may well see a three-headed snake vow to "stop 'em, tromp 'em, and crush 'em" three times and hear such statements as "one of the nice things about being evil is you get to lie a lot" ("The Great Gladiator Gig"). The program relies on verbal insults, such as calling someone a "clog in the drainpipe of happiness" or "belch brains." That's hardly the behavior or language that our society deems appropriate for most business, social, or family situations.

The Gang at Full Force

The most common social group depicted on Saturday morning TV is the gang. It may be a gang of humanoid figures, or of animated human figures, or of animals. A strong message is conveyed that gang association and gang action are legitimate and even glamorous.

What distinguishes a gang from a normal group of friends?

First, identity with and loyalty to the gang override any other loyalty, specifically that to family or society as a whole.

Second, gang members are all within a fairly narrow age range, whether they are teens or preteens.

Third, the older wizard for the group, whether it is a street-smart teenager leading children or an aged friendly scientist, is never a family member.

Fourth, the gang is identified by wearing a common uniform or emblem. Slogans and secret code words are often employed.

And fifth, the gang has a turf. With the turf comes the obligation to defend it at all costs, even to the cost of life.

"Teenage Mutant Ninja Turtles" falls nicely into the long legacy of gang profiles, which had as its origin the programs of the 1970s: "Yogi's Gang," "Superfriends" (Superman, Batman, Wonder Woman and Aquaman teamed together), "Fat Albert and the Cosby Kids," and even the animated version of "Lassie."

The basic plot line for "Teenage Mutant Ninja Turtles" is that four ordinary turtles are accidentally dropped into a sewer manhole, where they encounter a radioactive goo that causes them to grow to human size and gain the power to speak. The mutated turtles are adopted by Splinter, a similarly mutated rat.

Splinter had been the pet of a ninja warrior, and he continues to battle against his former master's nemesis. Splinter names his adopted sons Leonardo (the leader), Raphael (the rebel), Michaelangelo (the prankster), and Donatello (the whiz with anything technical). He drills them to become ninja warriors, which they are by the time they reach teenager status.

As a gang of four, they have a look, a code language and mutual love of pizza, a shared religion (ninja), and a wise older guide who is not part of a true family unit.

Most cartoons today are based on the concept of a peer group: "Shirt Tales," "Getalong Gang," "Snorks," "Mighty Orbots," "Smurfs," and even "Alvin and the Chipmunks." They all have one thing in common: it's important for each member of the unit to work, think, and operate as a group (or gang) member. The concept of individual winning and losing, much less individual identity, seems to be losing fast.

Where is the family? For the most part, the family doesn't exist on Saturday morning. When one is depicted, the relationships are trivial. In cases of impending tragedy or trouble, parents are never around or never consulted. The child must save himself, his family, his neighborhood, his nation, and sometimes his universe. Generally only other children are his allies, fellow conspirators, or fellow heroes.

The child as savior is a troublesome concept. In the movie *Willow* and also in the video of *The Never-Ending Story,* the message is just that: a child can save us all. Many cartoons place that burden on children.

Two of a child's prime fears are that his peers won't like him or accept him and that he will be left alone. These fears often take the form of a child's being afraid of being laughed at, taunted, rejected, and so forth.

The importance TV places on gang association does little to allevi-ate either fear. Indeed, the evidence leads one to believe it more probably fuels these fears.

In addition to emphasizing the importance of peer associations, TV holds up model children and says, "Be like him. Wear this. Play with this. Own this. Have fun with one of these. Eat this. Behave this way. And if you don't, you're a nerd."

Furthermore, TV promotes the idea of being with people. In real-ity, TV viewing is a loner's activity that actually separates children from other children.

In a study with five- and six-year-old inner-city boys, Murray (1972) found that heavy TV viewers were most likely to have prob-lems of social adjustment and to be interpersonally passive, less persistent, and more shy. How ironic that such a child spends his days watching people who are just the opposite of that profile!

What makes an emotionally healthy youngster?

A child needs to keep in touch with reality, above all. A child has a tendency to fantasize, which is a normal behavior that serves use-ful functions. The adult role, however, is constantly to pull that child back to reality so the child can learn how fantasy and reality relate. Discipline sets boundaries. Children need them.

A child needs to be around people who will show repeatedly that they accept him for who and what he really is, not what he might be or should be.

A child needs praise for her accomplishments. She needs to hear approval when she succeeds at tasks and to hear approval all the time for the fact that she is.

Television cannot give a child any of these things. It promotes fantasy as reality rather than differentiating the two. It cannot pro-vide praise as feedback. It cannot say to a child, "You are good enough."

College freshmen—a group of people raised on TV and subject to virtually every statistic presented in this book thus far—were re-cently asked in a survey to list their strengths and weaknesses. On the average, students listed six weaknesses for every strength. Talk about lousy self-esteem!

Where did they get such a negative image of themselves? Not from loving parents. More than likely, they got it from The Box.

So What's a Parent to Do?

Ask your child these questions as you watch TV together.

1. Is that character a real character or something made up?

2. Is that person on the program real, or is it an actor playing a part?

3. Could that event really happen? What would be the result if it did? Follow up by asking, What's the worst thing that could happen to that character on TV? What's the best thing?

4. Is that setting real, or is it a model, an imitation of a real place, or something made up in someone's imagination?

Continually give your child a reality check! Explain the truth when her answers reflect fallacies.

If your child's eyes are glued to TV, you have an added challenge as a parent to make certain his feet are touching real ground!

Chapter Seven

TV as a Sex Educator

For your obedience has become known to all. Therefore I am glad on your behalf; but I want you to be wise in what is good, and simple concerning evil

(Rom. 16:19).

Habitual Saturday morning TV viewing sets in motion the pattern of watching TV in the morning. Most children don't know or care what day of the week it is. They like to watch TV on Tuesday morning as well as they like to watch on Saturday morning—which they do, in droves.

But on weekday mornings, they encounter daytime television, otherwise known as the soaps. Nearly four dozen network broadcast hours a week are turned over to daytime serials. Along with them come at least ten hours of commercials each week. Soap operas air to a viewing audience of 18 million people every day. About a fifth of those watching are children.

What are the primary messages of soaps?

While soap operas appear to be centered on families, and on family relationships, the families are often dysfunctional. Sometimes they are embroiled in illegal activities and violence, for which they are rarely imprisoned. Family relationships, especially marital relationships, are sketchy at best. Disposable marriages and disposable love affairs are far more common than happy marriages.

Children featured as part of the plot line are generally presented in terms of an unwanted pregnancy, a crisis (accident or illness), or a custody battle. Rarely are they shown on camera. And rarely is any interaction shown between adults and children that might be considered normal everyday behavior. Furthermore, the human development process is depicted as anything but normal. Growing up is portrayed as being fraught with danger.

To children in need of stability and trust, this depiction of family life is anything but reassuring.

The presumed audience for the soaps is female, likely to be a wife and mother, and perhaps a grandmother. The hidden audience,

however, is the child at home. This year the average American child
will see 9,300 sexual acts on TV and hear nearly 65,000 sexual innuendos. Nearly 95 percent of all sexual acts will be acts of fornication
or adultery.

Once again, TV isn't portraying reality. Some fairly recent
surveys and studies indicate that most sexual acts among adults (in
some studies, more than 95 percent) take place within the context of
marriage.

The references to sex, of course, extend into evening programs,
also watched by children. Diana Workman and Kim Bloomfield, in a
late 1986 study, monitored ten popular shows and counted the
number of physical, verbal, and implied acts or references to sex.
Most programs were aired during family viewing time. They found:

- 24.5 acts per hour of touching behaviors, including kissing,
  hugging, and other affectionate touching

- 16.5 acts per hour of suggestions and innuendo involving flirta-
  tious behavior or general allusions to sexual behavior

- 6.2 times per hour when discouraged sexual practices, from sa-
  domasochism to exhibitionism, were suggested

- only 1.6 times per hour when educational information about
  sex was presented

Virtually every program they monitored included at least one sexual reference, and they found that many instances were on sitcoms
where the sexual reference was intended to provoke laughter.

They also noted that children, especially boys, are often the
straight men in jokes about sex and sexuality; that TV children
avoided discussing problems in general with their parents and sexual problems least of all; that sex and sexual issues were usually
presented in a way that exploited at least one character involved;
that tender, loving sexual behavior was rarely portrayed between
people in committed relationships; and that the subject of birth control was generally avoided.

Many sexual references also simplify and objectify love, or even
define love as sex. Perhaps no place is this more obvious than in
music videos, a favorite of children.

In a 1984 study by Sherman and Dominick, reported in the Winter 1986 *Journal of Communication,* the researchers concluded that adolescent sex on music TV was long on titillation and physical activity but devoid of emotional involvement.

And on Saturday morning, your young daughter may see Jem kiss her boyfriend. Your children may see Orco become ecstatic over a kiss from She-Ra.

Your son may have seen heavy sexual overtones on "Robotech." Its plot construction, including the sexual references, was similar to that of a soap opera.

Are children influenced by these sexual references? Yes! Parents often forget that children are sexual beings. They can be aroused easily and influenced to dwell on sexual content.

In 1987, 1,700 seventh- to ninth-graders in Rhode Island were interviewed. The findings were presented by Jacqualine Jackson Kikuchi at the National Symposium on Child Victimization, April 29, 1988:

- 24 percent of boys and 16 percent of girls said that it was acceptable for a man to force a woman to have sex with him if he has spent money on her.

- 65 percent of boys and 47 percent of girls said it was acceptable for a man to force a woman to have sex if they had been dating more than six months.

- 87 percent of boys and 79 percent of girls said rape in marriage is permissible.

- 31 percent of boys and 32 percent of girls said it would not be improper for a man to rape a woman who has had previous sexual experiences.

- 50 percent of the students said that a woman who walks alone at night and dresses seductively is asking to be raped.

These are the attitudes of twelve- to fourteen-year-olds who are about to begin dating. Where but by watching television could they possibly have been introduced to these ideas with such consistent repetition that they have adopted these views as their own opinions?

On one hand, we tell our children and teens to avoid getting pregnant; yet we feed them a steady diet of sexual messages. We're truly creating the onset of early puberty, as one educator described it.

Consider the evidence: one million teenage girls (nearly one in ten) will get pregnant this year.

So What's a Parent to Do?

If your answer is yes to any of these questions, turn off the program your child is watching.

1. Are the female characters wearing clothing that you would not like for your children to wear?

2. Are the women viewed as objects to be used?

3. Are there sexual innuendos or overt sexual acts?

4. Is the program sexually arousing?

5. Are women characters harmed more often than male characters?

Chapter Eight

Attention, Shoppers!

He who has the gold, rules.

—A variation on
the Golden Rule

Hedonism: "pleasure or happiness is the sole or chief good in life."

—Webster's Third New
International Dictionary

A TV watcher is a true consumer of TV only if he or she is watching a pay-TV program. In most cases, the TV watcher is actually the product. The viewer is being sold to advertisers.

Cy Schneider, a former ad man who worked on the Mattel toy account and who served as vice president and general manager of "Nickelodeon" for six years, said, "Those who think the primary purpose of children's TV is to educate are wrong. All television is a business. Its purpose is to corral an audience to watch commercials" (*L.A. Business Journal,* May 1987).

To this end:

- Children will see more than 350,000 commercials by the time they are 18 years old.

- According to the American Academy of Pediatrics, before a child enters kindergarten, he has seen 75,000 commercials.

- Current levels of advertising allow for 14 minutes per hour of advertising on weekdays and 11 minutes per hour on weekends.

- Commercials occur on Saturday mornings at a rate close to 20 an hour.

- The average child will see 78 commercials on Saturday morning. On one Saturday morning in the late fall, we counted 60 commercials for toys.

- Half of all children's advertising is for junk food. That amounts to about $700 million in commercials to promote snack items, candy, and sugar-coated cereal.

We as parents must never forget that TV is big business. Lots of dollars change hands, and advertising budgets are higher than most of us can imagine. The power of the medium is such that the big bucks are warranted.

Mattel, for example, discovered that power of television-based advertising in 1955 when it launched its first major TV ad campaign. Virtually overnight, the $500,000 company became a $12 million one!

In 1990, Disney and its Buena Vista subsidiary spent about $60 million in marketing support for their movie and video titles and another $30 million in advertising.

RCA/Columbia planned to spend $10 million just for the marketing and advertising of the movie *Ghostbusters II*.

Are children really watching the commercials? Early studies reported that one- to ten-year-olds watch commercials about 40 percent of the time and eleven- to nineteen-year-olds about 55 percent of the time. Younger children watch the commercials more on Saturday mornings than they do during prime time.

From these studies, one might conclude that children do not watch. However, the level of viewing for commercials is nearly the same as the level of viewing for programs.

To be sure, children are a more fickle audience for commercials than adults are. Advertisers and TV producers know this well. Advertising aimed at children must be stronger than that aimed at adults mainly because the child isn't the purchaser. She must be convinced to become an active lobbyist for the doll or breakfast cereal she wants.

Advertising aimed at children is also rooted in urgency, the don't-delay-get-this-product-today message. The reason relates to the short-term memory development of a child.

Commercials make good use of repetition. The average number of repetitions—fast-paced cuts from one scene to another showing children eating the product and so forth—in food commercials is nearly four verbal and more than four visual repetitions per thirty-second commercial. Some commercials show more than ten repetitions.

Commercials also rely on unusual visual effects to command and hold a child's attention. Such visual effects include mingling animated figures with real children; speeded-up camera action; and camera techniques that may transform objects or make them vanish in thin air.

Research studies show that dramatic violence isn't necessarily a plus for advertisers; yet Schuetz and Sprafkin (1979) found 113 aggressive acts in a single Saturday morning sample of 414 commercials. The amount of aggression in the commercials was about three times that found in the programs surrounding them. The greatest concentration of aggressive acts was found, in all places, in the cereal commercials!

Children report that they especially like commercials that have humor and are entertaining (Atkin 1975; Ward 1972).

Commercials use the technique of rhyme to maximum advantage. Jingles are very effective.

The goal of advertisers is to get a child to remember the name of the product and then to desire it. That's really all advertisers aim at in selling to children.

Can children routinely recall the name content of commercials? You bet!

In one study, 400 children were given 15 minutes in which to list all the products they could remember from their general experience of watching TV commercials. Some were able to write down as many as 50 products, including 15 brands of beer.

The National Science Foundation (NSF) and the Federal Trade Commission (FTC) both have concluded from their studies that children learn from advertisements. Moreover, they learn precisely what the manufacturer wants them to learn: name brands.

Your Child as Product Lobbyist

Advertisers advertise products to people who have little discretionary income and, many times, no financial power whatsoever and no ability to buy. Why? The advertisers know that your child is being used as a product lobbyist.

From 1973 to 1978, the Gene Reilly Group, Inc., produced a report titled "The Child." It was made available to major TV sponsors who were advertising to the children's market, and it sold for $15,000 per issue. The contents were not made available to public organizations, such as ACT, or to the government. It was a document for corporate eyes only: Burger King Corporation, Campbell Soup Company, General Mills Incorporated, and so forth.

The report drew this conclusion, among others, for these clients:

> Mother can simply be a "purchasing agent" for the child. So it is important to know not only what the young child buys, and why he buys, but it is also of crucial importance to know what purchases the child influences, how he or she influences, and what responses such influence attempts are likely to receive. (1973 report, p.3)

Advertisers have spent hundreds of thousands of dollars to answer those questions.

Advertising research conducted by Helitzer Advertising has revealed that parents will pay 20 percent more for an advertised product that their child suggests, even when a less expensive or nonadvertised product is no different, assuming that the parents have not already made up their minds definitively about the product choice.

Helitzer Advertising also surveyed mothers and found that they spent an average of $1.66 more per week at the grocery store when their children asked for specific products and brands. Carry that out to its logical conclusion and one quickly sees that literally billions of dollars are added annually to grocery retail sales.

Little information about the products themselves is included in the commercials aimed at children. It's difficult to tell what a toy is made of; price is never mentioned; often no hint is given as to how, exactly, the toy works.

What is emphasized is the appearance or the action of the product. Children are repeatedly shown how much fun it is to play with a toy or to eat a product.

How often do children ask for the items they see advertised on TV?

Atkin asked three- to twelve-year-old children this question in a

1975 study and found that 28 percent said "a lot" and another 55 percent said "sometimes." When it came to breakfast cereals, 33 percent said "a lot" and another 45 percent said "sometimes." Mothers who were asked to report their viewpoint gave almost identical responses. Furthermore, those who watched more TV were more inclined to ask.

In one study, 25 percent of heavy TV viewers reported that they ate Sugar Smacks a lot, compared to only 13 percent of the light viewers. Nearly half of the heavy viewers ate Hershey bars a lot, but only a third of the light viewers did so. Overall, the amount of TV viewed was directly related to the amount of potato chips, soda pop, hot dogs, and general snack and processed foods consumed.

And what are the attitudes of children who are denied the products they ask for?

In one survey conducted two weeks after Christmas, 35 percent of the children polled said they were disappointed they didn't receive certain gift items, and the rate was higher for heavy TV viewers than light viewers (Robertson and Rossiter 1976).

Another group of researchers asked children how they felt toward parents who didn't buy for them what they had seen on TV. Thirteen percent of the children said they felt negative feelings a lot and another 38 percent said they felt them sometimes. When it came to cereals, 20 percent said they got mad a lot and another 25 percent said sometimes. Again, heavy viewers responded to the "a lot" category more than light viewers. The parent who doesn't buy is often seen as a culprit.

The child bombarded by commercials often demands toys, cereals, or other items. He truly feels they are part of his rightful domain on this earth. When that happens, a certain delight is taken out of the realm of play and toys. Certainly, a sense of thankfulness is also removed when a child has internalized the commercial message that he needs a toy and that by giving him one, a parent is only fulfilling his job, just as if the parent were giving the child a bottle of milk.

In making our claim that children learn from TV commercials, we must also point out that children do not necessarily learn all from commercials that the advertiser or the parent wants them to learn.

Cereal manufacturers have argued for years that they show their

products with juice, milk, toast, and so forth, and that they therefore promote the idea of a balanced breakfast.

A formal study by Atkin and Gibson in 1978 asked children about
balanced breakfasts, and researchers found that nearly two-thirds of
them couldn't recall anything having been said about a balanced
breakfast even though an audio disclaimer on the commercial they
had seen clearly used those words. Two-thirds of the children had
no idea what the term *balanced breakfast* meant!

One small boy viewed a commercial that showed a couple driving
their new luxury car and then showed them in a beautiful picnic
setting, seated cozily on the ground with their lovely car in the
background. When asked what the commercial was about the boy
responded, "It's a good idea to go on picnics. They're telling people
to have more picnics."

Even such a miss in understanding the content of a commercial,
however, underscores a basic premise: commercials are good at selling an attitude. If they can sell the concepts of new, fun, exciting,
and even picnics, that may be enough.

A ray of good news may be that children can also learn positive
messages from public-service announcements when they are well
done and when they use the same techniques as commercials. Messages about such behaviors as cooperative play, good nutrition, not
littering the nation's highways, wearing seat belts, and not using
drugs or smoking have shown positive impact on children's attitudes and behavior. In other words, children didn't just know they
were supposed to buckle up, and they didn't just have a better attitude about wearing a seat belt; they were actually buckling up more
on their own (Atkin 1978). (In chapter 5, we discussed other positive
messages that can be learned.)

It's important to know who is advertising, what is being advertised to your child, and how firms are going about it.

Who is advertising to your child? To some degree the answer
depends on which station is being watched. On network affiliates,
your child is more apt to see commercials for cereals and candy (and
other sweets and snack foods) than any other item, including toys.
On the independent stations, however, nearly half the commercials

are for toys, and only about a quarter of the commercial time is for cereals and candy combined.

Who are the biggest advertisers to children in terms of amounts of money spent on commercial time?

- toy manufacturers and retailers such as Hasbro and Mattel
- fast-food chains such as McDonald's and Burger King
- Cereal and candy companies such as Kellogg's, General Mills, and M&M/Mars

If one watched television only on Saturday mornings, one would conclude that Americans eat only sugar-coated foods. More than 80 percent of the food products on network-affiliated stations are for manufactured food products, the majority of which contain a high level of sugar. Natural foods such as fruits, vegetables, meats, and dairy products rarely are advertised. Nutritional information rarely if ever is provided.

The trend changes as Christmas approaches. During October and November, your child will see a great many more toy commercials, probably up to 50 percent of the commercials aired.

Food and beverage commercials are more likely to be aired in the summer months.

Do children really understand that commercials are attempting to get them to buy something? In several studies, children were asked questions such as Why are commercials shown on TV? or What are commercials trying to do? (Bever, Smith, Bengen, and Johnson 1975; Robertson and Rossiter 1974; Sheikh, Prasad, and Rao 1975; Ward, Wackman, and Wartella 1977).

Virtually all these studies found that children under eight years of age can't explain the selling intent of commercials. Younger children simply don't understand the basic nature of a commercial. They don't understand that the commercial is designed to sell a product or to influence them. The commercial to them is simply one more sequence of visual cues presented in an ongoing wave of visual cues.

Only when children reach second or third grade can you safely assume they understand that the purpose of commercials is to get people to buy things. By the time they are twelve, the majority of children know that commercials are for selling and that many of the claims are exaggerated. But even then, a percentage of children still do not perceive the selling intent. Most of the children who know claims are exaggerated know this not from their sophistication in analyzing commercials but from having owned products that didn't live up to the televised promises.

An older child may have seen through some of the exaggerations on commercials aimed at young children, but he still believes the claims made for teen and adult products, whether soft drinks, cars, or laundry soap.

Licensing is ultimately the name of the game.

Consider just how lucrative licensing can be, especially when the product is linked to an animated or a dramatic children's series.

When the "Mickey Mouse Club" was revived in the mid-1970s, the Long Island company that held the license to produce Mousketeer ears was turning out about 40,000 pairs of ears a week. Within two months after the show began, the company was producing 360,000 pairs of ears, with an annual projection of 18 million pairs of ears. All other sales of licensed products jumped to the same tune. Perhaps no example of franchising outperforms the merchandising of Mickey Mouse and his Disney friends.

Mingling program content and commercials isn't a new TV trend. In the spring of 1969 "Romper Room" created a ruckus among mothers, who circulated a petition protesting the show's practice of having the host sell a line of Romper Room toys directly to the audience. Children, the mothers argued, couldn't tell the difference between the program and the commercial, and they took the host's opinions as facts.

The trend hit a new level, however, with the introduction of the "He-Man and Masters of the Universe" series. For the first time a toy line became a TV series. In addition to the toy line, other items related to He-Man and the Masters were licensed.

By 1985, just three years after this intense cross-marketing effort began, more than $500 million of the He-Man toys had been sold each year by Mattel, which had also gained $500 million more annually in licenses.

G.I. Joe became animated, as did She-Ra, Transformers, Voltron, and so forth. Toy line after toy line became animated. Cross marketing was carried to the point where many began to call the toy-based series "commercialtoons."

Advertising on TV is big business; the world of licensing is even bigger. It is considered a $52 billion industry. And Bart of "The Simpsons" and the Teenage Mutant Ninja Turtles are making names for themselves in that industry.

Almost anything popular can, and has been, licensed. In some instances the animated figures in commercials have become stars in their own rights. Perhaps the most recent and best example is that of the California Raisins, who quickly became licensed as toys, and then had their own CBS half-hour special produced by Claymation.

Character figures have been used to promote a wide variety of products other than toys, too, reinforcing their presence and appeal to children. For example, Road Runner has promoted Purolator Courier, and Daffy Duck has been a spokesman for Nestle's Laffy Taffy products.

Still other promotional wrinkles are appearing on the horizon almost daily. Already, TV programs encourage children to call 900 and 976 telephone numbers to hear messages from Santa Claus or members of popular rock groups, or to hear a story about an adventure featuring a comic-book character. Some programs have even prepared a dialing signal that is transmitted over the TV set; the message to young viewers is to hold the telephone receiver near the set so the TV character can dial the number for them!

Children, of course, have no idea that the calls cost money. And even if they did know, they probably wouldn't care.

The Children's Advertising Review Unit (CARU) of the Council of Better Business Bureaus has joined a number of parent and consumer groups in expressing concern about these programs. They are strongly protesting the use of automatic tone dialing by means of TV-transmitted signals. They are demanding that the programs tell how much the calls will cost, and that any phone numbers be written on the screens, not stated auditorially, since small children have a more difficult time decoding and remembering written numbers. They are protesting the use of *now* and *only* as pitches on the commercials, and they are rebelling against programs that fail to clarify that the child is going to hear a story about a character rather than talking to the character directly. They want no programs to show cartoon characters or celebrities talking on the telephone, and they are calling for programs to eliminate any premiums and other direct-marketing promotions as part of the calls.

So much for protest. The programs, meanwhile, are becoming increasingly popular and are likely to be a major part of future interactive children's programming, with huge financial possibilities in cross marketing and licensing of products and characters.

What is the net result to children of this bombardment of licensed products and cross-marketing techniques?

To a great extent, the symbols and characters of TV become an even greater part of their symbology and their self-identity.

Educator Rose Goldsen noted:

> When the children are not watching the shows, studying the stars, or playing with these dolls and games, they can sleep on sheets stamped with the same symbols. They can wear them as signs upon the bosoms of their T-shirts. . . . All these commodities, now, collect and concentrate the auras that surround symbols, and feed to children the very stuff that nourishes their minds. (29:271)

Children can no longer escape the TV culture.

The self-esteem of children is increasingly being built on superficial things. Children begin to draw their identities not so much from their families, their communities, or their cultures as from the things they own and wear.

If nothing more, we are raising children who are prone to consumerism as never before. The acquisition of things also looks far too easy, for the most part.

Children are growing up wanting their lives to be like, and to be spent with, television characters who aren't rooted in reality. They want to own what the characters own. Most of all, they want to own things for the sake of creating an identity that will ensure their acceptance by peers.

So What's a Parent to Do?

You can limit your child's viewing to public broadcasting, where the commercial messages are far fewer. Or you can limit your child's viewing to videocassettes.

You can protest. Edward M. Markey (D-Mass.) is a strong advocate in Congress for lessening the amount of advertising on children's programming. At this time he's chairman of the House Telecommunications and Finance Subcommittee. You can let him know how you feel about the fact that children's programs during the daytime have twice as many commercial interruptions as those on prime time.

(An entire list of organizations and addresses is provided in Appendix A.)

You can educate your children. Consumer's Union has released a film titled *The Six Billion $$$ Sell* to teach children about commercials and the techniques used on them. Vision Films has a similar release titled *Seeing Through Commercials.* Both are excellent and get the message across to viewers as young as second-graders.

One Home Box Office thirty-minute show, titled *Buy Me That!: A Kid's Survival Guide to TV Advertising,* was hosted by an animated character named Jim Fyfe. Its intent was to show children what happens behind the scenes during the making of commercials and to explain what various commercial terms such as "parts sold separately" and "some assembly required" really mean.

Dorr, Graves, and Phelps (1980) were pioneers in developing a program for schools in which teachers can teach children how to evaluate programs and commercials. The course includes such points as how plots are made up, how sets are constructed, and the fact that programs are broadcast to make money.

You can encourage your local school to rent these films and videos to teach your children about the commercials they are watching.

Visual literacy may well be one of the main courses taught to children in the coming decades, just as grammar and spelling are taught today.

You can support Act for Children's Television (ACT), an organization founded in 1968 to focus attention on children's programming.

As early as 1971, ACT called for three moves to be taken by the Federal Communications Commission:

1. Children's programs should not have sponsors or commercials.

2. Performers and hosts of programs for children should not be allowed to use or sell products by brand name on children's shows.

3. Each station (local) should be required to produce fourteen hours a week of children's programming, divided equally among preschool, primary, and elementary age groups.

You can applaud advertisers who take a stand against certain programming. For example, Toys-R-Us actually apologized for having sponsored an episode of "thirtysomething" (ABC) in which two homosexuals were portrayed in bed discussing their love life after having had sex with each other.

You can recognize that the problems associated with commercial advertising are only going to continue to grow. The infant and preschool market is presently about $1.2 billion strong at retail, and growing.

Chapter Nine

The Great Escape

It's easy to quit watching TV. I know because I've done it hundreds of times.

—A TV addict

I used to watch "Lucy" with the kids. I remember turning on shows I thought were OK for them to watch, and plugging them in. Then, I began to observe my use of television with the kids, and the way they were watching. My kids, when they watched TV, seemed different from when they played or slept. They looked hypnotized.

—Marie Winn, author
of *The Plug-In Drug*

By 1981, Gallup Opinion Index surveys revealed that Americans were spending 46 percent of their leisure time watching TV.

If you are a typical American adult, you watch between three and four hours of TV a day. The hours add up quickly: more than twenty hours a week, eighty hours a month, one thousand hours a year, and during an average lifetime, from six to eight years.

A recent Nielsen survey of American viewers stated that the average family is now watching TV seven hours a day. Nobody in the history of the world has been entertained as much as seven hours a day. The most ardent theatergoers and moviegoers would be hard-pressed to sustain seven hours a day, even for a week!

A key question we can all ask ourselves is this: Am I controlling the media, or is it controlling me?

What keeps Americans so plugged in to The Box?

For many children as well as adults, TV is an escape mechanism.

Every child faces a certain amount of anxiety about her existence and future. Children also learn young that the world is a place with lots of choices and lots of opportunities for failure. They feel anxiety about their chances for success and about whether the world will even be there by the time they reach adulthood.

TV is one way of avoiding that anxiety. Turn it on, tune out, and escape reality for awhile. But perhaps in avoiding their temporary anxieties, children may actually be trapped into a greater state of anxiety caused by a failure to discover who they are or what they are capable of doing as unique individuals.

Parents often tell me that their children seem to go into a trance when they watch TV. Other parents note that their children have a dull look in their eyes, as if they've been hypnotized.

One reason for this is that TV watching tends to disrupt the sleeping patterns of many children. Children who watch a great deal of TV often stay up late at night doing so.

Another explanation may relate to the fact that a hypnotic state is achieved, to a great extent, by having a person concentrate on the movement of an object with a fixed focal length, while he hears low soothing sounds. Objects are usually dangled in a slow rhythm to and fro, to and fro. How different is this from the average children's TV program in which the music underscore never quits, chase scenes carry the eyes back and forth across the screen, and the motion is constant?

What actually happens to a child's brain when he watches TV?

The steady impulses of the TV program itself—the constant motion, the change of scenes, and the resulting flashes of color every few seconds—cause the brain to release a chemical that, in pharmaceutical terms, would be considered a depressant. This brain-induced drug allows children to appear glued to a TV set, sometimes watching it for as long as three hours without a bathroom break. This is the same type of chemical that, when given in larger doses, can result in a drugged state often used for brainwashing purposes!

As children watch TV in this affixed state, they receive information on what is considered a passive level. They are not required to decipher the information as it is received. Little decoding is required in programs that are mostly visual, which is the case with cartoons.

The child receiving this stimulus in a passive state receives it largely with the right hemisphere of the brain. This hemisphere controls visual-spatial development; the left hemisphere controls verbal-analytic development. Thus, prolonged TV watching can actually stunt a child's developing analytic skills, which are the skills most required by school-related activities—reading, writing, decision-making, problem-solving—and even everyday conversation.

If you are thinking that we are drawing the conclusion that TV is, in and of itself, a drug that causes brain damage, you are correct!

Given a choice, most viewers will choose something that takes little effort to understand. In the same way that most people will choose to eat something that requires little effort to fix, such as junk foods, so TV viewers seem to gravitate toward junk TV. By junk we mean programs that have little prosocial value, that teach few new skills, or that provide little new information. Viewers also want something that will give them a laugh or a visceral thrill.

Television addiction is a possibility that more educators are exploring. To the addict, TV has become a way of escaping stress or the need to interact with other human beings, as well as a habit rooted in sensory arousal that makes TV watching just as difficult to forgo as the ingesting of heroin for a heroin addict.

For most children, TV is a fixture of life. They've seen it on in their homes more often than not since they were born. They've grown up with certain characters. They are media addicts without even knowing it.

In a *USA TODAY* poll, Americans recently listed media consumption as one of their most frequent activities, including listening to stereos, records, and tapes; watching cable TV; recording programs and viewing them on a VCR; and watching sports on TV.

Statements from those who consider themselves TV addicts are enlightening as to the effects of TV on the heavy viewer. Some have referred to it as a tranquilizer. Addicts report they feel a loss of control over their viewing. They just can't turn the TV off.

Most addicts report a feeling that TV no longer gives them satisfaction, even though they are watching more of it. The programs provide no pleasure but instead sap their energy and will.

Some report a total loss of a sense of time. They speak frequently of suddenly being aware that the late-night news is over, and they have no memory of how or why they spent the entire evening in front of The Box.

Nearly all addicts report that they structure their personal schedules around TV. They wouldn't dream of missing certain programs, no matter what the alternatives offered to them.

One study found that more than half of all elementary-school children questioned watched TV while eating their evening meal, and an even larger percentage watched while doing homework.

J. P. Robinson asked TV set owners and nonowners in eleven countries (the United States and Europe) to keep diaries. He found that sleep, social gatherings, conversation, household care, leisure activities such as knitting and writing letters, and newspaper reading all were activities that decreased for TV set owners.

Most addicts confess they watch too much TV and are angry with themselves for it, but they can't seem to do anything about it. Many report that when they try to quit TV, they experience withdrawal symptoms of extreme nervousness.

An escape that becomes an addiction?

The leap from using TV as a drug to using chemicals as drugs isn't a great one. Drugs are simply one further way of escaping, one more addiction.

Pete Hamill, in an excellent article titled "Crack and the Box" published in *Esquire* magazine, cited what he perceived to be a link between TV use and drug use:

> Television, like drugs, dominates the lives of its addicts. And though some lonely Americans leave their sets on without watching them, using them as electronic companions, television usually absorbs its viewers the way drugs absorb their users. Viewers can't work or play while watching television; they can't read; they can't be out on the streets, falling in love with the wrong people, learning how to quarrel and compromise with other human beings. In short, they are asocial. So are drug addicts. . . .

> There are other disturbing similarities. Television itself is a consciousness-altering instrument. With the touch of a button, it takes you out of the "real" world. . . . Each move from channel to channel alters mood, usually with music or a laugh track. . . .

> In short, television works on the same imaginative and intellectual level as psychoactive drugs. If prolonged television viewing makes the young passive (dozens of studies indicate that it does), then moving to drugs has a certain coherence. Drugs provide an unearned high (in contrast to the earned rush that comes from a feat accomplished, a human breakthrough earned by sweat or thought or love). . . .

> The drug plague also coincides with the unspoken assumption of most television shows: Life should be easy. . . . Life on television is almost

always simple. . . . And if life in the real world isn't that simple, well, hey, man, have some dope, man, be happy feel good.

Beyond its own nature as a drug, what does TV teach your child about the use of drugs (which may be interpreted as the use of virtually any substance that might give a high feeling)? Plenty.

In one episode of "My Little Pony" a character drank a potion, her eyes shot forth like lightning, she grew to enormous size, and she received power. What a drug trip! In another episode a character, acting in the role of savior of the kidnapped Ponies, stopped to get a piece of the rainbow from Mushram, where the wizard lives among the magic mushrooms. Magic mushroom is the name given by drug users to one type of highly hallucinogenic mushroom.

Perhaps one of the more infamous days in cartoon history is April 23, 1988. In an episode of "Mighty Mouse: The New Adventure," the cartoon hero is depressed because his girlfriend doesn't seem to care. He draws a handful of powder from under his cloak and inhales it. Almost immediately, he is back to his normal, happy self!

Viewers were outraged, and CBS responded by claiming that Mighty Mouse was snorting a mixture of flowers, strawberries, and over-ripe tomatoes. No mention was made of those ingredients, however, on the cartoon. Even if the substance wasn't intended to be cocaine, why did Mighty Mouse need to resort to snorting anything to regain a happy mood?

Do cartoon producers blatantly attempt to compel children to use drugs? Probably not. They gain nothing by being media pushers.

More than likely the acceptance and the use of drugs, and the accompanying culture, have been parts of the personal background of the writer or producer. Many persons in the TV industry are products of the drug culture prevalent in our nation during the 1960s. They openly admit to experiences with LSD, speed, and pot, and often point to their drug experiences and alcoholism as being influential in the development of their illustration styles and content today.

What about alcohol? As a part of TV commercials and programs, a child will see alcohol consumed 75,000 times before he or she reaches the age of twenty-one. Nearly 90 percent of the movies released in America show the use of alcohol. The consumption of alcohol in movies is nearly 1,000 percent more than that consumed in reality. More than 99 percent of those portrayals show alcohol in a neutral or favorable light.

According to a 1986 National Institute of Drug Abuse survey, the average child first consumes alcohol at the age of 12.3 years and tries marijuana for the first time at the age of 13.4. That's the average child!

A sixteen-month study on children and TV was conducted by a task force of the American Academy of Pediatrics. One finding, summarized recently in *USA TODAY,* was that "television encourages the use of drugs, alcohol and tobacco by glamorizing them. The heroes whom children emulate are often shown smoking and drinking beer."

A thirty-six-member commission composed of medical and educational leaders affiliated with the National Association of State Boards of Education and the American Medical Association recently issued these facts:

- Nearly 40 percent of high-school seniors admit to being drunk at least once every two weeks.

- Alcohol-related accidents are the leading cause of death among teenagers.

Not only are we teaching children about drugs on Saturday morning and at other times, but we are giving them a drug of sorts to prepare them for later chemical drug use. The compounded effects are staggering and frightening, and they show no signs of diminishing. Perhaps the war on drugs actually needs to start with TV!

So What's a Parent to Do?

Ask yourself honestly if your child is watching too much TV.

Does she come straight home from school and head for the TV set?

Does he spend all of a sunny spring Saturday morning in front of TV?

Does she watch TV before school?

Does he frequently say he is bored?

Does she consistently choose TV over other activities?

Does he watch TV during mealtimes and while doing homework?

If the answers are yes, make a move to wean your child from TV. Limit the viewing time. Make it a strict rule. You may need to drop just one hour a day for awhile, and then drop another hour, and so forth.

Set a good example. Find other things to do besides watch TV. Invite your child to participate.

Watch programs with your child and discuss them, including any instances you see of alcohol or drug use. Point out the fallacy of the glamour that may be attached to the chemicals' use.

Finally, talk to your child about drugs. The Box already has.

Chapter Ten

The New Catechism

Whatever things are true, whatever things are noble, whatever things are just, whatever things are pure, whatever things are lovely, whatever things are of good report, if there is any virtue and if there is anything praiseworthy—meditate on these things

(Phil. 4:8).

More than four million hours of programming a year are broadcast for consumption by the American consciousness. To a great extent, TV has become the religion for the masses. How can we make that claim?

To begin with, it is nearly universal in its use by the culture. In the same way that citizens regularly go to the church or synagogue of their choice on Sunday mornings or other set times in the week, so some Americans today feel compelled to sit in front of their TV sets on Monday nights.

Its use in the home and in a person's life is ritualistic. How many meals will be consumed sans TV in American homes tonight?

It prescribes behavior. It defines sin and goodness. Whereas religion is based on a code of acceptable behavior, TV tells with its own definitions what a person should do in certain circumstances.

It tells what products a person should consume. In the same way that a religion often prescribes dietary laws and promotes concepts of abstinence, moderation, and sacrificial giving, so TV has dietary laws (food rich in sugar) and promotes the concepts of consuming to the point of gluttony.

In the same way that religious teachings give definition to the word *conscience,* so TV today gives definition to the word *conscious.* Viewers today are conscious of a great deal they might never have experienced otherwise.

Religion establishes order and justice in a society; it reinforces the concepts of law. Television establishes a new order based on power and, to a degree, intellect. The more powerful forces win on the police shows; the more clever person wins on the game shows.

The main difference probably is this: religion tends to limit behavior and what a person sees, does, and says. Television tends to have few limits.

The catechism is also vastly different.

Today's children are enrolled in a catechism that promotes Eastern religions, new-age philosophies, neopaganism, and the occult.

Thirty years ago, most children were growing up in a culture that could be considered Judeo-Christian. Today's children are growing up in a neopagan culture.

Many parents will rebel at that thought. But stop to consider all the messages being foisted on your child.

Today's cartoons are filled with religious propaganda. That may not bother you if you are a follower of Eastern thought, Hinduism, new-age philosophy, Zen, or a participant in occult practices. Unless, of course, you are a strong adherent, and then you should be leery of the place given to competing viewpoints.

If you are an atheist, you should be concerned. Your child is being fed a steady diet of religious symbols.

If you are a Christian or an orthodox Jew, take heed. Your child is being taught something that is the opposite of what you believe!

Much of religion has to do with the issue of power—what it is, who has it, how one gets it, and how it works.

A child's perception of power is tangible. "Mine," says a child. "Yours," he may have to ultimately admit.

The perception of power on today's cartoons is quite different. The power has a spiritual source: a supreme power, a force, an entity beyond the person who or which causes that person to have power or not to have power. The power is absolute. It possesses. It controls.

Virtually all Eastern religions claim that spiritual power lies within. It is the force that compels one toward some type of self-realization or self-actualization.

Nearly all Eastern religions are rooted in the idea that the person is his own savior and his own supreme being. Qualities of spiritual greatness lie within and need only to be released. How they are released forms the basic doctrines and variations on the theme.

Christianity advocates that spiritual power is resident in God and that God's presence and power can be invited to indwell a person through believing in Jesus Christ, repenting of sins, receiving the

Holy Spirit. Christianity provides for a free-will acceptance of God's power into one's life.

Occult practices, or satanism, recognize a power outside the individual, and adherents call upon it for wisdom and guidance. This power is considered resident in Satan and his demon cohorts. Once a person has been possessed by demonic power, however, the person no longer is capable of exerting his will over the evil working in his life.

Both Eastern religions and occult practices employ a variety of symbols, myths, and methods that often overlap.

To understand what is happening on Saturday morning television, and its ultimate spirit-and-mind-controlling influences, we need first to understand something about these symbols, myths, methods, and the religions that arise from them. We'll consider four main religious orientations, all of which have abundant manifestations on Saturday morning television.

Spiritism is the oldest form of religion on earth. Virtually every religion today, other than Judaism and Christianity, had its origins in Babylon. The seven basic principles are these: there is a supreme father; all men are equal brothers; life is a continuous existence; man follows an endless progression; a person's walk along that path is his or her responsibility; communion with spirits can help; and there will be rewards someday for those who follow good. Most spiritists choose Satan as their father and demons as their consulting spirits, and they believe the path of life is one of reincarnation. Today, nearly 750,000 people are avowed spiritists in the U.S., about one-third of the world's known adherents.

The Hinduism active in America today is not the same religion as that founded five thousand years ago along the banks of the Indus River in Persia. Today, Hinduism seeks to include all religions in some type of oneness. The way to gain knowledge is through mystical insight, which comes by way of devotion and a general disinterest in things of this material world. Modern Hindus believe not in a single God but in the idea of gods in everything and in a rather amorphous universal god spirit that can pervade all substance.

The religion has given rise to TM (transcendental meditation), a spiritual form of yoga. A major sect of Hinduisim is ISKCON (the Hare Krishnas).

Hinduism holds generally that anyone is capable of becoming enlightened to the point of being a god, and that reaching this state is something man is responsible for doing on his own.

It allows the worship of a wide variety of deities.

Zen Buddhism, or simply Zen as it is called in America, is derived from the Japanese branch of the meditation school of Buddhist philosophy. It was introduced into Japan from China in the seventh century. More than 300,000 Buddhists are active in America today.

The teaching, in a simplified overview, is that life is filled with sorrow and suffering, and that through the processes of reincarnation, a person can move from sorrow to a state of nirvana, which may be nothingness or perfection depending on the branch of Buddhist thinking. One can move closer to nirvana by following the Eightfold Path: right belief, right resolve, right word, right act, right life, right effort, right thinking, and right meditation.

To follow this path, one calls on his spirit within, and that alone. An individual is totally responsible for his own salvation; there is no such thing as sin because there are no absolute standards for holiness.

The new-age philosophy holds to one main overriding belief in wholeness, unity, and peace. Many of its symbols, practices, and buzz words are grounded in the belief that out of fragmentation, one might find or achieve oneness.

Friendship is essential to achieving unity and a one-world environment. All must be friends and cooperate. (The message is repeated too many times to count on children's programming today.)

Visual conditioning is important. Many symbols are used repeatedly, including all-seeing eyes; circles and triangles in various combinations; rays of light; rising suns; and crosses with diagonals placed against them. The rainbow is perhaps foremost. New agers believe that each color of the rainbow represents a god responsible for a certain human personality activity or trait. From a Christian context, the rainbow has a different meaning as a symbol of God's covenant power with man never again to destroy the world with a flood. To a new ager, the rainbow is connected to the idea of antahkarana—the building of a rainbow bridge, generally between mankind and the over-soul of man, often named Lucifer, the light bearer.

To fly to this new unity, new agers readily use the symbol of a Pegasus (winged horse) or the unicorn.

One can get to wholeness or holism by means of yoga, music meditation, psychic healing, macrobiotics, dreams, biofeedback, reflexology, self-help methods of visualization, mind control, TM, positive thinking, and hypnosis.

Each of these four religious orientations is aimed at achieving a new world order. Most seek some means of raising the consciousness of the individual. Many recognize or employ the value of such occult practices as:

- astrology
- fortune telling
- palm reading
- ascended masters
- the force
- astral projection
- numerology
- necromancy
- parapsychology
- the third eye
- tarot cards
- Ouija boards
- spirit guides
- magic
- levitation
- mental telepathy
- wizardry
- spiritism
- clairvoyance
- extrasensory perception

Overriding all these activities and beliefs is a general humanism, declaring man as the supreme being. Humanism always holds that man is capable of self-fulfillment, of generating peace on earth, and of conducting himself in right ethical conduct solely by his own efforts and without recourse to God.

Appendix B is a fairly comprehensive list of occult symbols and terminology. I invite you to study it carefully as a reference point for watching today's cartoons.

You may not think your child is watching any of these things on Saturday mornings or on children's programs. Pay close attention, then, to the following discussion.

The Hallmarks of Paganism

We must not overlook general paganism as a whole. Paganism contends that gods can be linked to human beings, and that they intermingle with human beings to influence human affairs.

One of the most common figures of ancient paganism is the mother-goddess figure. She became Venus to the Greeks and has also been known as Ishtar, Cybele, and Artemis. Another common figure is the half-human, half-animal figure. Dagon was a famous ancient half-beast, half-man god; Horus was a popular hawk-headed god.

At this point, let's jump into the Saturday morning ghetto and see what we find.

We find "The Wuzzles," all of which are hybrid creatures, two animals in one (for example, Rhinokey, Hoppopotamus). Scales, a character on the "Go-Bots," is half machine and half serpent. By adding machines to the mix, neopaganism has a lot of room for variety in its god figures!

"Thundercats" features six cat-people. They live on the planet of Third Earth, which is totally unpredictable, with both good and evil using occult powers. The main evil character is Mumm-Ra, a living mummy; his intent is to rule Third Earth, and he has scores of demons to do his bidding.

She-Ra's very name is taken from Ra, the god-queen of ancient Egypt. Ra, or Isis, was called the Queen of Heaven and was worshiped by apostate Jews as part of their Baal worship.

Masks were important to pagan peoples. In many primitive societies, masks represented more than a change in one's appearance. Masks had a direct link to the world of spirits; they were considered a channel by which men could tap the forces of the supernatural. Many people who attended witches' sabbath services during the Middle Ages wore masks to hide their identities. Masks often have been worn throughout history at funerals to hide the identity of mourners so that the dead might not execute any retribution or harm.

Masks are equally important to neopagans today. It is easy to view the fantastic quality of many cartoon superheroes as people wearing masks.

Many cartoon characters, He-Man and She-Ra included, employ this concept of masking. Adam is ordinary until he takes on the persona of He-Man; Adora is ordinary until she takes on the persona of She-Ra.

The ability to transform is also a pagan feature. It is a variation of the idea that one might assume a separate identity under which to operate.

The forerunners to the children's programs that feature such transformations may well be "Jeannie the Genie" (1973–75) and "Sabrina the Teenage Witch" (1969–72). Together, these two programs dominated the Saturday morning time slot for more than 300 showings between 1969 and 1975.

Today's everyday transforming girl is a character named Jerica who becomes Jem when she twists her magic earrings and says, "Show time synergy." She can project a hologram of herself anywhere she desires.

The transforming power of the "Supernaturals" and "Visionaries" was especially spooky, for they transformed not into superhumans but into spirits.

Shamanism is the official term for practices in which a spirit guide is consulted for wisdom. It is characterized by a belief in an unseen world of gods, demons, and human ancestral spirits. The shaman's guardian spirits were considered to be the spirits of his ancestor. A *shaman* is a "priest who uses magic for the purpose of curing the sick, divining the hidden, and controlling events" (*Webster's New Collegiate Dictionary*).

An abundance of spirit guides appears on children's television. He-Man and She-Ra have theirs. BraveStarr has one, who goes by the name Shaman. Lion-O of "Thundercats" has Jaga.

The images of snake and dragon also are prominent in paganism, and now neopaganism. Mumm-Ra, of "Thundercats," has fiery serpents coming from his head, with two black snakes coiled and poised for striking in an emblem on his chest and as part of his headpiece.

In most instances, the dragons are envisioned as friendly ones. As one character says in the movie *The Never-Ending Story* (Warner Bros.), "Having a luck dragon with you is the only way to go on a quest." Also in that children's movie, viewers will see a medallion of serpent figures intertwined that gives supernatural power to its wearer.

The serpent and the dragon, of course, have long been symbols for Satan.

The unicorn and the winged horse (Pegasus) are common neopagan symbols. They are derived from Greek and Roman mythology, where they were generally ridden by gods and goddesses.

Pegasus received his power to fly when he was fitted with a golden bridle. It was his job to take lightning bolts and thunder to Zeus.

The unicorn and Pegasus have appeared generously over the years in association with the new age movement, also called variously by such names as the golden age, age of Aquarius, and eon of Horus. The idea is that the new world order can be ushered in on the wings of innocence and gentleness.

The unicorn has been a popular symbol since medieval times and is believed to have magical and healing powers. It is a symbol of transformation, the idea being that the unicorn, with a whole, unified, single horn, represents the creation of a holistic social order. Unicorns are frequently coupled with rainbows, a symbol discussed earlier.

The underlying rationale for the colors of such cartoon characters and toys as My Little Pony, Rainbow Brite, Gummie Bears, and Care Bears is rooted in the concepts of rainbows, unicorns, and flying horses. Children playing with these toys and watching these programs readily pick up the idea that the various rainbow personalities are good and helpful, and that the rainbow bears a power to transform situations magically.

Familiars—animals bestowed with a demonic spirit power to assist a person in supernatural activities—are common in virtually all pagan and occult practices. Cats, especially, are common familiars. For thousands of years, cats have been worshiped as deities or cursed as demons. The cat was sacred in ancient Egypt. To the Druids, cats were human beings who had been transformed as a result of evil powers. In West Africa, some primitive religions view cats as the recipients of human souls after death. Black cats especially were adopted by the occult.

It's difficult to watch children's TV and movies, older Disney movies included, without finding cats in the role of familiars. He-Man's familiar is, indeed, a cat named Battle Cat.

Familiars have moved beyond cats, however. BraveStarr and She-Ra have horses, and the ghostbusters have their own pet ghost.

In paganism, and neopaganism, grimoires—occult books of incantations and spells—are frequently consulted.

Various graphic occult symbols also appear regularly on children's programming. The circle is a common symbol often used in an occult manner. In both Indian folk and satanic practices, dances and rituals are generally performed inside a circle, the center of which is considered the place of the great spirit.

Often the circle is divided into two segments, signifying dark and light, cold and heat, male and female, good and bad, and so forth. The yin/yang symbol is one example.

Triangles, especially in relationship to circles, are also common. Ceremonies are considered threefold activities, with the participant, the medium (priestess, witch, and so forth), and the spirits all working together.

The number four is considered by many occultists to be the most sacred number. It can represent the four quarters of the earth, the four winds, the four seasons, or the four elements (earth, air, water, fire).

The number seven also is referred to frequently, especially by Indians. The Sioux have seven sacred rites, for example.

Pentagrams definitely are an occult symbol and represent Satan.

The colors red and black often are used in an occult way and, when linked, can indicate sacrificial or occult rites.

Look for these numbers and geometric shapes as we discuss cartoons in greater depth over the next few pages.

Occult practices also are something to watch for as we detail the content of some of the foremost cartoon series.

Scrying, which means seeing, is a common occult practice. It generally refers to seeing into the future. This type of divination generally uses transparent materials such as water, crystals, mirrors, or crystal balls. One entire episode of the "Super Mario Bros." featured the Brothers' consulting a fortune-teller.

Astral projection is the process by which a human being projects himself or herself into a figure of light, generally through space to a location some distance away from the true location of the person. To the medium who is able to perceive this image, the figure projected often appears as if it were in a cloud or as a form in smoke, flames, water, or mirrors.

The third eye is part of a Hindu teaching, which claims that every person has a hidden third eye in the middle of the forehead just above the point where the eyebrows meet. This eye is considered the seat of supernatural sight, clairvoyance and, ultimately, power. The Eye of Thundera is similar to what the Hindus call this third eye or all-seeing eye. It is prominent on "Thundercats."

Necromancy is perhaps the blackest of the black arts. It literally means communication with the dead for the purposes of divination.

The Babylonians, and even the Sumerians before them, believed they could find out about the future by studying all sorts of happenings—the shapes that cracks took in a clay brick wall or the movement of animals across an open field, for instance. Before any major decision could be made, they sought out omens.

The practice of necromancy and divination is common in today's cartoons, both on TV and in the movies. Time and again, animated characters consult signs before taking action. A noted example of necromancy is the communication between Little Foot and his deceased dinosaur mother in *The Land Before Time*.

An old and persistent belief exists in cultures around the world that everything has a real name that enshrines its essence and ultimately is that thing. Men and women have attempted to learn and to pronounce the real name of a person or animal to experience power over it or to adopt its power. Words are, from this perspective, weapons of power or tools of power.

Language also is a prime tool of sorcery, mainly through incantations. Incantations, as such, can also result in divination. They have become a common feature of many animated series.

Lion-O of "Thundercats" asks for power by saying, "Give me sight beyond sight," as the crystal on his sword becomes a third eye.

BraveStarr summons his shaman by bowing his head and praying, "Shaman, I need your help. Thank you for coming."

Possession is also an occult phenomenon. In cartoons, possession often is indicated by glowing eyes. Frequently, the eyes glow red. Possession also can be represented by displays of fire, such as lightning bolts flowing from a character's eyes or hands.

Occultists generally view the following as the eight means by which a person might become fully realized as a medium, witch, or priestess.

First, the use of dance or ritualistic movement. The Super Mario Bros. have their own dance, by the way; you can do the Mario. Barbie also has a dance.

Second, the use of wine, incense, drugs, or other chemical inducements that can cause the spirit to be released. Caldrons of brew are common on cartoons.

Third, the use of meditation and concentration, especially staring at mental images, whether imagined or real.

Fourth, the use of language in the form of rites, charms, spells, and runes.

Fifth, scourging.

Sixth, controlled breathing and other forms of physical control, such as lowering blood pressure or increasing blood flow.

Seventh, the great rite, which is ritualistic sexual intercourse.

Eighth, achieving a state of trance or astral projection.

Bear these eight points in mind as we discuss several cartoon series.

"BraveStarr"

"BraveStarr" is a combination of space-age and western adventures. The discovery of rare and expensive Kerium, a chemical supposedly used for powering spaceships, causes a boom in New Texas, a wild, lawless planet. The program is set at Fort Kerium some time after the Great Kerium Rush of 2349. The good citizens request a thousand marshals, but only one is sent: BraveStarr, the "toughest lawman in the Western Galaxy."

BraveStarr has an ally (a familiar) in Thirty-Thirty, his tough-talking horse. Thirty-Thirty goes through transformations similar to those of his rider. He can become, through magic, a horse-man that walks upright and carries a futuristic shotgun named Sara Jane. The female judge in the series is named JB, and there is a cute deputy named Fuzz. Together, they fight the Tex-Hex and his forces.

The main evil force behind Tex-Hex is Stampede, whose logo is the skull of a bull. Tex-Hex is actually a spirit being that looks like a living skeleton with glowing red eyes. Tex-Hex can transform himself into a demonic cloud that can rematerialize anywhere he chooses.

Absolutely no attempt has been made to hide the occult imagery of this cartoon. In "BraveStarr," your child will see a wizard who hypnotizes and a shaman called Shaman who communicates from the flames of a campfire, as spirits come up from the fire and surround him. In an episode entitled "Balance of Power," you'll hear, "With magic, I cure magic."

In "Strength of the Bear," the shaman teaches BraveStarr and children to "face your darkest fears," to recognize that courage and intelligence are their greatest powers, and to have faith because "the spirits will provide for you."

The general teaching is given frequently on the series that good people come in all shapes, including alien and demonic ones.

"She-Ra—Princess of Power"

"She-Ra—Princess of Power" is the story of Adora, who is one of the Friends of the Great Rebellion, engaged in fighting the Horde that has taken control of the planet. Adora becomes She-Ra when she holds her sword aloft and cries the incantation, "For the honor of Greyskull."

The Rebel Force, of course, is a good force because freedom is the goal. Its members are heroes solely because they are freedom fighters. The moral is starkly drawn that it is okay to fight if one fights for something considered good.

She-Ra rides Swift Wind, her horse (familiar), which also bears magical qualities. Her sword has the capability of transforming itself into a wide variety of weapons solely by word command from She-Ra.

She-Ra often consults her medium or wizard, Light Hope, for advice. Her shaman is called the Sorceress, who appears in the crystal stone of She-Ra's sword.

Shadow-Weaver, who has the capability of disappearing and leaving behind her shadow to talk to She-Ra, is the evil force. When evil characters call upon her, they use the title Blessed Mighty One and chant, "Come darkness, come trouble."

On the series "She-Ra," your child will see such things as a winged dragon, with two horns on its head and one on its nose; characters translated by beams of light, which are triangular in shape and come from a circle on the floor; enemy robots swallowed up by the earth, which gapes open after a spell is cast; Shadow-Weaver doing magic by consulting a large occult book called *The Ancient Book* for formulas; brown demons rising from brown ooze; and a monster who reads minds.

White magic is applauded on "She-Ra"; black magic is not. In one segment ("Talent for Trouble"), children are taught that magic can be messy and unpredictable, however.

She-Ra has healing powers among her magical gifts. In one segment, she heals Scruffer, a combination lion and unicorn, by laying her finger on his leg.

In "She-Ra" you'll find such teachings as these:

- Power comes from the light of the ethereal moons
- Trolls are good guys, rejected by humans
- Taking opportunity quickly is the trait of a good warrior
- "You must do what you know in your own heart is right"
- There must be only one ruling power on a planet.

As in "BraveStarr," friendship and courage are critical. The ultimate wrong is for a person to stop loving. In one segment of "She-Ra," the title heroine even goes so far as to cry for her enemy because he was given the gift of life and has wasted it; therefore, when he dies, no one will care.

"The Real Ghostbusters"

"The Real Ghostbusters" series is an animated spin-off of the popular movies released under the *Ghostbusters* title. In the series, there are four ghostbusters (all men); the woman secretary is a rather dizzy character.

On this series your child may well see such things as nails, cars, a refrigerator, and a steel girder that all become possessed ("Lost and Foundry"); a mighty battle between the forces of good and evil held at Jaguar Baseball Stadium, where the players meet once every five hundred years to play for one soul; and a computerized spirit guide ("Bird of Kildarby").

In one episode, the ghostbusters declare, "I want to open diplomatic relations with the spirit world," and they affirm that a "good scientist is open to everything." A number of derogatory comments are made about children in this episode ("The Revenge of Murray the Mantis") by the way.

The ghost in one episode has eyes that glow red. After several encounters with the ghost, one ghostbuster declares, "It's a miracle we're all right." Another one responds, "I don't believe in miracles. I believe in luck." The episode concludes with the message that there is a happy little kid inside all of us, including a happy little kid spirit inside a ghost. The other message is that it's wrong for the ghostbusters to compete against one another since that is a violation of friendship, their highest trait ("Ghostbuster of the Year").

"He-Man and Masters of the Universe"

In this blockbuster series, already referred to several times in this book, Prince Adam, who is something of a wimp, is transformed into He-Man simply by raising his sword and uttering the magic incantation, "For the power of Greyskull." He is thereby transformed into the one man who can get the job done, anywhere, anytime. He is the brother of She-Ra and was the first of the siblings to appear on TV.

He-Man battles against the evil Skeletor, who shares his goal: to get into the Castle Greyskull to obtain all the wisdom of the Council of Elders. The difference lies in their motives. Skeletor wants the wisdom for evil purposes, He-Man for good. The methods they use, however, are highly similar. The satanic nature of Skeletor is not hidden. He even hisses when he speaks.

References to the reliance on brain power, with Greyskull's being in the shape of a human skull, and the release of all power from the brain are definitely neopagan.

Cringer, Adam's cat, becomes Battle Cat (his familiar). Man-at-Arms is Adam's shaman. Teela is the Warrior Goddess. Dressed in her cobra collar and breastplate, she is reminiscent of ancient Buddhist statues.

Skeletor is frequently pictured, especially in the comic books related to the program, sitting in a classic lotus position, with palms uplifted, levitating with a crystal ball floating nearby. He gets his evil power from a pyramid. Among his powers are the abilities to astrally project and to read people's minds.

One can't help noticing that the action in "He-Man and Masters of the Universe" is nearly constant, and that the music track runs simultaneously. The technique only adds to the hypnotic effect of the series.

As a further note, "He-Man and Masters of the Universe," "She-Ra—Princess of Power," "The Real Ghostbusters," and "Brave-Starr" all are the creation of one company—Filmation.

"Care Bears"

The "Care Bears" animated series evolved from a greeting card series that spawned a toy line that turned into a movie, which in turn spun off the TV program. The message of the Care Bears on the surface is a cozy one: you care about your teddy bear, and it cares about you.

The Care Bears live in Care-a-Lot and have names and corresponding symbols that depict their natures. All the Bears are different; yet they are all really the same, say the narrators of the show, because they care.

Friendship once again is the supreme character trait. The show emphasizes feelings. The prime feeling, of course, is love.

The Bears tell little stories that have sharing themes. For example, in one episode the Man in the Moon sends bright moonbeams to bring all the Care Bears together ("Care Bears Bedtime Story").

So what could be wrong with such a cuddly lot? When they are animated, they weave a subtle message filled with magic, humanism, the practice of transactional analysis, Bahai beliefs, and the notion of spirit guides. The Bears are cute, but new age nonetheless.

"Dino-Riders"

The Dino-Riders are a group of future-time human heroes who become involved in a galactic battle with a group of monsters and are then moved through a time warp back into prehistoric time on earth, along with their enemies.

The monsters, called Rulons, address their leader as "lord," "brain box" some of the dinosaurs to gain control over them, and make such statements as "I want the pleasure of this kill myself."

The Dino-Riders wear crystals that, when they glow, help them engage in telepathic communication with animals and with one another.

One of the most amazing things about these programs is that the good guys never get hit and neither do the foremost bad guys. The Dino-Riders might win a battle but never the war. The Rulons always live on to fight another day.

The characters have such names as Quest Star and Young Star. Their dinosaur friends are plant eaters. The meat eaters are those captured by the Rulons.

Lord Koulos is the chief Rulon, and his associates are called, appropriately enough, Vipers.

"Teenage Mutant Ninja Turtles"

The Turtles' origin was described earlier in this book, so we will isolate a few examples from the TV series and the movie.

In the animated series, Splinter frequently is shown in a classic lotus position, with a large yin/yang symbol behind him on the wall, as he counsels the Turtles.

Ninja is based on an ancient religious practice called Kung pau in the cartoon. In history, this early religion, which employs one of the earliest mind-control techniques known, is called "kujucurry." Splinter often lays his hand on his head as he communicates with the Turtles, indicating a mind-control technique at work.

The ninjas were trained to be assassins; in their practice of ninjitsu, they seek to train their minds and spirits, as well as their bodies, to become fighting tools. A foremost technique is hypnosis. They form signs with their fingers to hypnotize, and when they reach perfection in their religion, they believe they gain the eyes of god, which allow them to foresee future danger.

Early episodes of the Turtles were violent but rather campy in their story lines and uses of language. Increasingly over the years, however, the religious undertones of the ninja belief have become more obvious.

The Turtles' recent movie was rated PG, but the day I saw it in a theater outside Dallas, at least half the audience was in the three- to six-year-old range. The movie is filled with curse words, has a reporter who dresses like a hooker, and is extremely violent.

The children that day saw mental telepathy exercises while the turtles were in meditative positions with legs crossed, hands raised upward, thumbs and forefingers looped in the classic lotus position; the image of Splinter appearing in a flame that changed color to blue as the Turtles, who are calling him forth, increase their powers of concentration; and Turtles endowed with power after an intense spiritual experience in which they gain the psychic ability to fight successfully even when blindfolded.

"Casper, the Friendly Ghost"

The "Casper, the Friendly Ghost" series was one of the first to reference the occult. It appeared in the late 1950s. Its theme of ghost behavior is from the occult; yet most parents find the program cute for their children because it's rooted in friendship. The series frequently draws the conclusion that friendship is a beautiful thing, the implication being that friendship with ghosts is included. Under the guise of appearing harmless, little Casper opened the door to a closet filled with characters far more obvious in their evil.

The strong message of the "Casper" series is that ghosts are nothing to be afraid of. In point of fact, the occult is something that every person should be afraid of, if not for religious reasons, then certainly for reasons rooted in the future of our nation. Occult practices have no good result, either for an individual or for a community. They often lead to the most hideous forms of abuse, violence, and death. For those involved, delusion is a common result. Overall, those who practice the occult rarely strive to achieve anything based on real work. They often deny their parts in failures, always self-justifying their acts.

"Smurfs"

Papa Smurf of the "Smurfs" is a wizard who casts spells and mixes potions. He often refers to Beelzebub in the cartoons. *Beelzebub* literally means "lord of the flies" and is one name of Lucifer or Satan used in the Bible. Papa Smurf practices sorcery and witchcraft to help the Smurfs whenever they have a problem.

Occult symbols are used in numerous episodes. For example, in one episode Gargamel, the evil wizard, draws a pentagram on the floor and lights a candle at each point. He then dances within the pentagram while chanting a spell. When he finishes, a magical book opens across the room. A spirit leaves the book, enters Gargamel's body, and suddenly Gargamel has the power to do battle with the Smurfs.

It's difficult to imagine a more clear-cut portrayal of occult rites.

Beware These Shows!

The nine series discussed ever so briefly are certainly not the only ones that parents should be aware of as they allow their children to watch Saturday morning television and after-school syndicated cartoon shows. The list could go on and on.

Here is just a partial categorization of the shows to look for.

Witchcraft, sorcery, and magic

"Archie Comedy Hour" (with Sabrina the Teenage Witch)
"Bewitched"
"Blackstar"
"Defenders of the Universe"

"Dungeons and Dragons"
"He-Man and the Masters of the Universe"
"She-Ra—Princess of Power"
"Smurfs"
"Thundercats"
"Thundar the Barbarian"

UFOs

"Battle Star Galactica"
"Buck Rogers in the 25th Century"
"Dr. Who"
"Lost in Space"
"My Favorite Martian"
"Robotech"
"Star Trek"
"The Young Sentinels"

Gods, goddesses, and genies

"I Dream of Jeannie"
"Jeannie"
"The Secrets of Isis"
"Thor"

Spirit guides and new-age practices

"Care Bears"
"Ewoks"
"Shazam"

Martial arts

"Chuck Norris"
"G.I. Joe"
"Rambo"
"Teenage Mutant Ninja Turtles"

Metaphysics and lycanthropy

"Drak Pack"
"Fang Face"
"Go-Bots"
"Munsters"

"The Incredible Hulk"
"Transformers"
"Ultra Man"

The supernatural

"Casper, the Friendly Ghost"
"The Real Ghostbusters"
"Scooby Dooby Doo"
"Space Ghost and Dino Boy"

Magic Posing as Reality

"But what's the real danger here?" you may ask. The danger is that magic poses as reality on children's programming.

Leading occultists do not differentiate white magic from black magic. They perceive only magic. The Bible also makes no distinction between white and black magic.

Gone is the notion of once upon a time, which is a sure-fire cue to a child that he is embarking on a fantasy. The Masters of the Universe book titled *The Revenge of Skeletor* begins this way: "Deep in the farthest reaches of space, in another dimension of time and reality, there exist two worlds which orbit the same sun. One of these planets, a place of wonderment and beauty, is Eternia."

A child has no way of knowing that Eternia does not exist! It is postured as a real place.

It is impossible for a child fully to differentiate what is sacred from what is not. To a young child, attendance at church or synagogue is not meaningful most of the time. It's a time to sit still and be quiet in a fairly large room filled with adults. Music happens. An adult talks. Occasionally there are refreshments of some sort during or after, sometimes also known as Communion.

The value of the church experience is that, through repetition and time, the child will come to attach meaning to the symbols encountered. The same process works in the same way on TV.

Children's TV programs increasingly make no clear-cut distinction between the methods used by the good guys and the bad guys. That readily leads a child to assume that the methods are all neutral, or good. The arsenal of weapons employed by both good and evil characters includes psychic powers and occult symbols.

The animated series "Blackstar" was one of the most occult programs to enter the children's market. The symbolism in the name alone provides a clue as to the occult nature of the program. John Blackstar, the protagonist, has a Star Sword he uses for good in his battles with the Overlord of the Underworld, who possesses a Power Sword. Actually, the two swords are halves of one greater sword, which holds the power of a universal force.

There is really no way to know why Blackstar is good and the Overlord is evil. They both use the same techniques. They both seek control. Blackstar is handsome, and Overlord is ugly. Perhaps that's the telling difference.

In the program a child will also see Mara, a scantily clad woman with power to levitate objects and people. She is called the Enchantress and is a good character. Blackstar flies about on a reptile-like fire-breathing horse with bat wings; his name is Warlock. One can gain knowledge in this series by eating the nut from the Sagar tree, but this brand of knowledge results in good.

Who's the good guy again?

The danger with using occult measures to overcome villains is that justice is portrayed as being held in check only by supernatural power, not by judicial laws and procedures normal to our society.

Thundar the Barbarian, the hero of the program by the same name, opposes evil but uses the same techniques—mystical signs, symbols, and powers—as the evil ones he battles. The program is filled with wizards, and the message is that sorcery and other occult practices are acceptable if they are used by people with good hearts.

Many occult cartoons hide behind the face of cute.

In addition to the "Care Bears" and the "Smurfs," what could appear cuter than the "Gummie Bears"? Consider, however, what happens to them when they are animated for Saturday morning television.

One of the five Gummie Bears is a magician. The history of the Bears and all the spells they can use are contained in the *Great Book of Gummie.* They are descendants of the Great Gummie Bear, but since most of the bears seem to have lost their magical powers, they have been brewing Gummie Berry Juice, which gives them superhuman powers for centuries. Even a human boy becomes superhuman and is able to battle his enemies successfully after he drinks the magic juice. The enemies of the Gummie Bears always are ogres led by an evil, exiled duke.

Although the toys are cute, the stories on the cartoons are filled with magic and occult symbols.

Consider "Rainbow Brite," featuring the little girl by the same name. She, too, is a cute character, often seen gliding through the air on her flying horse.

What happens on Saturday morning when she is animated? She lives in Rainbow Land with her friends, the Color Kids, and the Sprites, the happy little workers who mine and make Star Sprinkles. Rainbow Brite's job is to keep the world light and filled with color and happiness. Of course, she is often confronted in her job by horrifying monsters, who at times are intensely violent. The rainbow, however, has the power to overcome evil.

Not only do these shows confuse good guys with bad methods, but they also emphasize power: the ruling, controlling, we-will-wipe-them-out kind.

Every child seeks mastery over his world and desires to hold his own against persons older or bigger than himself. The difference on these programs is that the power is absolute, it is universal, and it is a peer-group activity. Above all, the power is rooted in and available through the manipulation of symbols.

We cannot overestimate the value of the symbols on these programs. Every day of our lives, certain symbols help us understand patterns of behavior, institutional forms, attitudes, and values. Symbols become the very fabric of our soul language. They unite the intellect and emotions to create a semblance of discipline.

People often genuflect to a cross when they enter a church. The response has become a conditioned one. It has meaning, however, at both mind and heart levels, and that is why it is considered important and why it evokes a response. That response, over time, becomes a habit or a discipline. And eventually it becomes sacred.

The manipulation of symbols, therefore, becomes our religious lexicon. The manipulation of symbols gives rise to our spiritual language.

Myths, too, have great power. Myths pinpoint the mores and values of a society and pass them from generation to generation, from adult to child. They portray how a person in a culture should act and what she should hold important.

Myths do not provide a theory of life that can be adopted or discarded at will. They compel a response from us. They bridge our hearts and our minds, our intellect and our emotions. They create a visceral feeling, call forth a response, and cause us to think about consequences related to that feeling.

Myths are always rooted in history. They are the past calling out to the present.

The myths we present to our children today form the fabric of the values held by tomorrow's society.

Our concern also is that children can participate, and are participating, in a spiritual reality without their knowing it. It is our contention that when children imagine and role-play that they have occult power, they actually open themselves up to the acceptance of an occult mind-set.

Children may not understand the full meaning behind all the images and rituals they see, or even those in which they participate, but they are becoming familiar with them, accustomed to them, and will be less likely as teens and adults to see anything wrong with them.

What children see on TV gives them a mind-set—the attitudes, and the social-interaction behaviors—that will affect what they choose to learn and how they will choose to learn in the classroom and, ultimately, how they will choose to live. As we have discussed before, the real educational value of TV lies in the teaching of attitudes and values.

Children respond emotionally, not rationally, to the cues of TV. They aren't in a position to clarify their values. They are still developing a value system.

It is an adult's job to help a child develop a value structure, not to confuse the issue with mixed signals. At no time is it more important to draw the difference between good and evil with bold black-

and-white strokes. When you feed children mixed signals and gray messages, they are likely to experience value confusion all their lives.

The religious and value message of today's TV is that, above all: confused.

So What's a Parent to Do?

If your answer is yes to any of these questions, turn off the program.

1. Are there demons, spirits, or familiars that help certain characters achieve their goals?

2. Does the program have wizards, witches, or spirits as good guys?

3. Does the program have occult symbols, such as pentagrams or goats' heads?

4. Does the program portray occult practices, such as seeing into the future, levitation, mind control, divination, communication with the dead, and so forth?

5. Do the characters use the tools of witchcraft or the occult, such as wearing amulets, holding wands or staffs with magical powers, or consulting books of spells?

Our children are being taught by TV today to call on demons for power.

What if one answers?

PART

3

Saturday Afternoon . . . and Beyond

Young Child turns off The Box. Today's lessons are over.

Young Child moves outward into his world, to check the hypotheses he has just encountered.

And what does he find?

Reinforcement.

Young Child goes to the Toy Chest. Why, there are the same figures he just saw on The Box. *I'll bet they can act just the same way,* Young Child thinks to himself. And sure enough, they can.

Young Child goes down to the arcade. *Yep, they're here, too,* thinks Young Child as he sees the same characters act the same way they acted on Saturday morning. No point in going all the way to the arcade, then. Let's just bring the video games home.

Young Child turns to the bookshelf in his room and to the comic books under his bed, only to find the same characters performing the same stunts of bravery and violence, the same occult and magical practices, and spouting the same messages about sex, drugs, and the world at large.

Young Child goes to the movies. Sigh. Once again.

Layer upon layer. Concept upon concept. Values upon values. Behaviors upon behaviors. Symbols upon symbols. Again and again.

Young Child draws a conclusion.

The Box must be reality after all.

Chapter Eleven

A Trip to the Toy Chest

See Dick. See Jane. See Dick and Jane watch cartoons on television.

See Dick and his Transformer Action Figure, complete with automatic ion pulse gun and deflector shield. See Jane and her Shish Kebab Beetlejuice Action Figure with Scary Skewers. (Caution: Not recommended for children who still put objects in their mouths.)

See Dick's Transformer hit Jane's Beetlejuice doll with the ion gun. (Each sold separately.) See Jane hit Dick with her Beetlejuice Phantom Flyer Vehicle. ("Squeeze the handle bars together and stun obnoxious humans with the wheel bomb.")

See Spot run away from home. Run, Spot, run.

—**Melissa Morrison,**
The Dallas Morning News
June 3, 1990

Toys help a child play. While that may seem like an oversimplification, it's a fact many toy purchasers and toy manufacturers seem to overlook. Toys aren't simply for setting on a shelf; they aren't for looking at; they aren't for collecting. They are intended to help a child play.

When children play, they learn. Toys are the true textbooks of early childhood. Every toy teaches a lesson. In fact, toys are the tools that children use for learning about themselves and their environments. Toys show children what they can do. Toys develop motor skills and mental skills.

When children begin to play with toys, they generally are interested first in the nature of the toy itself. They want to see what it is and then what it can do. They touch it, pull it, probe it, sit on it and, if it's small enough, often try to bite it. They want to explore fully the limits of the toy in relationship to their bodies.

As a child grows, he begins to see toys as a means of expression. A symbolic language is attached to toys. Once this symbolization ability appears in a child, she plays with toys in a different way. Suddenly toys start to stand for something. He stacks the blocks up not just to see how high the stack can get but to build something. She no longer holds a doll just for the comfort of holding a plush, furry, cuddly something, but because the doll has a personality, a name, and embodies a relationship with her.

Toys help a child differentiate objects. They teach a child how to combine objects. They show a child patterns of sequencing and relationships in size.

Children project themselves into toys that will give them an opportunity to role-play what they will be as adults. A child bestows upon a toy life, character, ability, talent, and a setting in which the toy might exist.

People around the world use toys to teach their children about adult roles and adult behavior. One famous illustration of the use of toys in primitive cultures describes the training of children in the Cantalense subculture of Guatemala.

A Cantalense girl is given a water jar, a broom, and a grinding stone as toys. Each is a miniature version of those used by her mother. The Cantalense boy is given smaller versions of the tools used by his father, and he accompanies his father to work. Both boys and girls learn by watching their parents and then imitating them with their toy tools.

In our society, we provide toys of similar nature, although they are less likely to be exact miniature replicas. We give our children toy kitchen ensembles. We give them tractors to pedal and dolls to place in carriages.

More often than not, we find that when children play with these toys that mirror the tools their parents use, they mirror the appropriate behavior patterns for using the tools and also the specific personal characteristics of the adults they watch.

Toys are best when they have both play value and creative value.

By play value, we refer to the attraction of the toy, often measured in the amount of time a child will spend with it. Crayons, for example, have great play value for children of many ages. A child can color and draw with them for hours. A jack-in-the-box has less play value as a child grows older. It is cute the first time. But after four or five minutes of cranking to watch the clown appear, a child often is ready to move on to something else.

By creative value, we mean the ability of the child to use the toy to make up his or her own stories. Blocks and Tinkertoy-style building units have great creative value because of the many ways in which they can be used, all of the building designs being derived from the child's imagination. A toy is considered a hit when children keep discovering new things to do with it.

Imagination at work! That makes a good toy. But most toys associated with Saturday morning and weekday afternoon syndicated children's programs aren't good toys!

Consumer Reports puts out a toy buying guide that rates toys according to play value, educational value, and durability. By play value, they are referring to how much fun the toys give a child; by educational value they are referring to the degree to which a toy teaches skills and promotes learning. Action figures as a whole are about average in play value and durability but generally low in educational value.

Battle Beasts, for example, have been given a play value of 54, an educational value of 13, and a durability value of 66, all on a 100-point scale. By comparison, Lego Basic Building Sets have a play value of 90, an educational value of 84, and a durability rating of 93. And crayons (the standard-sized ones) score a play value of 83, an educational value of 75, and a durability rating of 60, largely because they get used up.

When children play with a toy, they are generally willing to suspend all disbelief; children believe in what they are playing. We have come to call much of play make-believe because of this very tendency. When children play, however, that play action is real to them.

What happens if a toy has occult symbology or has been designed to be used in a way that has occult overtones? Again, the child suspends disbelief and begins to believe in what he or she is playing.

If TV programs teach children the concepts of levitation, mind control, and astral projection, what do you suppose the children do with the toys based on those programs when they play with them? They pretend to engage in the same practices of levitation, mind control, and astral projection. And later, on the playground at school when the toys are nowhere to be found, what do children pretend in their playtime? Levitation, mind control, and astral projection!

We must remember once again that, like TV, the toy industry represents big business. The toy business last year topped $8 billion. And that didn't include games or video games.

Most toy manufacturers don't care much about what your child does with a toy or what your child learns from it. They are concerned primarily with the fact that you buy the toy in the first place. Their goal is to position a company's toy line in the overall market and then promote it.

It's difficult to find a toy product these days that doesn't have a line of related products and accessories. Most action-figure toy lines have between four and twelve figures. You can get seven figures for "Star Trek: The New Generation" based on those characters who appear in the new TV series, not the old one. The Robocop action dolls feature six good guys and four bad ones.

Nobody can top Barbie for the number of accessories available, but Golden Girl comes with a more varied wardrobe. Some outfits are of full battle regalia and others are evening gowns.

Barbie, by the way, has made the top-10 toy hit parade every year since 1964, according to *Toy & Hobby World* magazine. The doll was introduced in 1959, and more than 500 million dolls have been sold.

Buying a Barbie is a little like buying a house. The original purchase price is only the beginning of the expense. Barbie must have clothes, shoes, and other accessories. She must have friends, lots of friends, who in turn need clothing. She certainly needs a car, and a house, and a boyfriend who has a car and lots of clothes.

Toy marketers have discovered that a child who buys into a series will generally buy an average of $72 worth of figures and accessories in that series. Those are expensive toys!

This pattern of purchasing multiple figures in a toy line is one more aspect of reinforcement for the messages that the child has received from the TV programs.

One of the foremost messages being reinforced by action-figure toys is that of violence or war. Between 1982 and 1987, the airing of wartoons —cartoons with fighting themes—jumped from 1.5 hours a week to 43 hours a week. Correspondingly, the sale of war toys increased 700 percent for that same five-year period. In the past decade, the sale of war toys in the U.S. rose more than 200 percent and now exceeds $1 billion annually. Some examples include the Lazer Tag toy, G.I. Joe toys, and Rambo-related toys.

This proliferation of war toys led the New York State Legislature to pass a bill that was signed into law by Governor Mario Cuomo on January 1, 1989. The law included the prohibition of "imitation weapons" made of any material that "substantially duplicates or can easily be perceived to be" an actual firearm or gun. Toy guns must be a color other than black, blue, silver, or aluminum, and marked with a nonremovable orange stripe one inch wide running the entire length of the barrel on the sides and on the front end. The barrels of the toy gun must be closed for a specified distance. Violations of the law carry a penalty of $1,000.

Apart from one's political beliefs about war toys, these action-figure toy sets are detrimental to a child's play and development in two ways.

First, they are rooted in the idea of games, not play.

Games and play are different. Games have rules; play is free-form. Games have goals; play is freewheeling, with no goal outside the activity itself.

From a child's point of view, games involve more stress. Games involve competition. They have winners and losers. The victory or loss is definitive. Action toys are strongly rooted in winning and losing.

"But that's life," a parent might say.

Not really. Few circumstances in life are grounded in absolute winning and losing terms. People win in varying degrees. They lose by degrees. And most people have a pretty good balance in their lives of win some, lose some.

Second, the play of action-figure toy sets is rooted in imitation, not creation.

Made-up games give children an opportunity to choose rules, which in turn helps them develop reasoning ability and the ability to weigh arguments. Made-up games also help children learn how to reach consensus.

Made-up games may be ragged around the edges, but made-up games also have more room for interruptions, digressions, disagreements over the fine points, and often acts of compassion. Such games are much more like real life than are prescribed games of any type, including those prescribed by action toys based on cartoons.

With action figures linked to TV programs, the play has already been prescribed. The object has been designed to exert control over the child, or at least over the child's enemy. Such a toy doesn't lend itself to a child's imagination. It comes from an adult's imagination and is then placed in a child's hand.

"But children could vary the scripts," you may say.

They *could,* but they rarely do. The figures are too precise and too detailed, and the behavior they have seen for the toy on TV is also too precise and too detailed.

Prescribing Aggression

The main script provided for these children deals with aggression.

In a year the average four- to eight-year-old will see 250 episodes of "war" on cartoons and 800 advertisements for toys that can engage in war behaviors. This is equivalent to 22 full days of classroom instruction.

On these wartoons, a hero rarely tries to see things from the opponent's point of view or attempts to settle problems peacefully. I can't recall one such incident in the more than 300 hours of cartoons I've watched during the past year.

War toys do not encourage conversation, either, which is a critical aspect to negotiation or compromise that we adults value so highly in our political and economic environments.

The message of the programs when coupled with toys and games is this: war is fun, war is a game, and if you're one of the good guys, you won't get killed.

Nothing could be further from the truth. War is hell. Good guys die.

Where are the studies that say violent toys and cartoons do *not* result in aggression? They tend to be funded by companies in the toy industry. Toy researchers, often funded by toy companies, tend to claim that injuries to children happen not because of substandard design, engineering, or manufacturing of the toy, but because children use the toy incorrectly. They rarely confront the idea of emotional damage or social damage. They are concerned almost exclusively with physical harm.

The majority of studies, however, point to great increases in a child's aggression as the result of playing with violence-based toys. Turner and Goldsmith, for example, found that play with violent toys was associated with twice the level of antisocial behavior as play with nonviolent toys. In a follow-up study, children who played with He-Man and Masters of the Universe action figures showed twice the instances of pushing, shoving, kicking, and arguing compared to their actions when they played with Cabbage Patch dolls.

The National Coalition on Television Violence (NCTV) reported in 1986 that it had reviewed thirty studies done by university researchers on cartoon violence. The studies involved 4,300 children in six nations, and twenty-eight of the thirty studies found harmful effects. It also compiled a series of eleven studies done specifically on war toys and toy guns and found harmful effects reported by all the study groups. NCTV also has done two of its own studies using preschoolers and comparing their play with Masters of the Universe and Transformers action dolls and with Cabbage Patch and Fraggle Rock play. The action dolls correlated with increased antisocial behavior every time.

Some people support the idea that modern animations and action figures are good triggers for a child's imagination and that they help a child think about different worlds and different eras.

That argument has two problems.

First, young children aren't aware that the animations are fantasy. They are reality as far as the children are concerned. The reality evokes feelings of fear, bewilderment, and visceral excitement.

Second, the meanings underlying the actions taken by characters on the program are not fantasy. Hitting, shoving, and other methods of demolishing a foe are real.

Still others support the idea that war play is acceptable since we live in a world where war exists.

We also live in a world where drug and alcohol abuse, sexual abuse, and child abuse exist. If a cartoon began to show story lines of these abuses, parents would be up in arms. (Well, perhaps.)

One mother said to me, "But if I don't give my child a toy gun, how will he ever be prepared to be in the military someday?"

I answered her, "The military has concentrated training programs for just that purpose. Let them educate your son when he's eighteen or older."

Some cartoons actually prescribe play rooted in psychic aggression. For example, the programs "Gotcha," "Photon," and "Lazer Tag" all featured characters who controlled, manipulated, or defeated others by using enhanced mental powers. Children who seek to model that type of aggressive behavior may actually turn out to be the most aggressive, and dangerous, of all!

A child often visualizes himself as a certain character. He believes that he possesses all the attributes and powers of that character as a part of his role-playing. Parents see this often with children who are playing house and pretending to be adults. Children are always comparing their role-playing to the real world they live in. They move back and forth from fantasy to reality in a testing process.

When children pretend to be mystical characters, however, they have no means of checking their characterizations against the real world.

When children play with toys (such as those from the Visionaries and Supernaturals toy lines) and pretend to be characters who engage in occult practices, they may find themselves engaging in a reality that neither children nor parents had anticipated.

Certainly a familiarity with the occult often leads children to experiment with other spirit toys. A popular toy being sold in toy stores today is the Ouija board, which is described in the *Dictionary of Mysticism* as "an instrument for communication with the spirits of the dead." Exactly what message are parents hoping their children will receive from those spirits?

What would likely be the combination of a war toy and a spirit-based toy? Probably a toy that depicts horror!

In the model division, Screamin' Products will sell you their Pinhead Cenobite model, taken from the movie *Hellraiser*. This is a twenty-inch vinyl figure. You can also get a Munsters hobby kit or kits to make your own Minatron, Cyclops, Godzilla, or Alien, complete with blood dripping from the mouth. And you can get a plastic ten-inch kit of a guillotine, just like the one in Madame Tussaud's Chamber of Horrors.

Exactly what are parents hoping their children will do as a result of playing with these toys? What values and behaviors are they hoping their children will learn?

Faint Hopes

The action-figure toy craze seems to be waning. Most action-figure toy lines seem to have a three-year lifespan.

We also can hope that children will get numbed by the onslaught of similar plot lines. As one buyer for a toy store said, "All the figures look alike, all have the same features, all present the same morality play of good versus evil, and the kids are just getting numb" (May 1987 issue of *Toy & Hobby*).

One can hope.

So What's a Parent to Do?

How should parents choose a toy? Here are some suggestions.

Take the stand that no child is qualified to choose his or her own toys. Choosing a toy is a parent's job. Children are too easily influenced by advertising, packaging, cartoons, and peer pressure.

A child has no basis for defining a good toy. To a child, both good and bad are initially fascinating. It's only after play experience that a child develops a sense of whether a toy is fun or boring, whether it breaks easily or lasts, and whether it's truly useful in exploring the world. You as a parent may not always guess right in your choices, but you'll come a lot closer than your child can.

Ask yourself, What is my child going to do with this toy? instead of What does this toy do?

The classic example of failure along this line must surely be the toy Teddy Ruxpin. Parents were fascinated with what the toy did. Children couldn't have cared less after they saw the mouth move the first couple of times. The toy failed because it left no room for the child's imagination, and parents were too often afraid to let the child play with the toy unsupervised because it was so expensive. Never buy a child a toy he can't play with!

Avoid toys associated with cartoons, movies, or TV programs. Give your child toys that do not have the script already written for their play.

Buy only toys that are kid powered. Avoid toys that allow the child to watch just another machine in action.

Look for toys that are durable, that will last longer than the box. Choose toys that can be cleaned and reused.

Choose toys that can be played with for a number of years and that are appropriate for the general age group of the child.

Choose toys that will build the values and behaviors that you want your child to have as an adult.

Few toys portray fatherhood. My Buddy is one of the few male dolls I've seen, and I heartily recommend it to the parents of preschoolers.

Why let your boy play with a doll? Or cook in a toy kitchen? Because those activities are a lot closer to what his real life will be one day than most of the other toys manufactured with boys in mind.

Few boys will grow up to be football players or soldiers. A high percentage of boys, however, will grow up to be fathers. All boys will grow up and keep their desire to eat, and many of them will need to know how to cook.

Avoid the impulse to buy your child too many toys. The quality of toys is what counts, not the quantity.

More than 60 percent of all toy purchases are made in the eight weeks preceding Christmas, according to *The Hume Moneyletter*. Make your Christmas list early; pare it down; and avoid overspending, overindulging, or overglutting the toy chest.

"But what should I do," parents frequently ask, "if I've already bought some of these action figures for my child?"

I suggest you buy them back. Don't take them away as a punishment. Admit to your child that you made a mistake and buy back the toy so your child can purchase, under your supervision, a good toy in its place.

Many times we have found that when a parent sits down to explain why a toy is now viewed as bad, the child will volunteer to throw it away.

What can you do to counter the effects of toys that your children's friends may bring to your home?

First, watch closely to see how the children play with the toys. Encourage them to add other props to their sets, including such common household items as colanders, empty toilet-paper rollers, Legos and other building blocks, and so forth. Encourage the children to make up new settings and to come up with new child-initiated plot lines using these sets.

Second, ask the children questions about the toys: What would G.I. Joe like to eat for dinner? Do they have that in the setting you've created? Where can he get it? Who will fix dinner for him? Who will eat with him?

Other parents say, "I think something should be done at the manufacturers' level."

We can ask toy makers and cartoon makers to emphasize creativity more than they do. Challenge them to base plots on problems in which characters can find novel solutions without resorting to aggression or occult practices.

We as parents must also regard this as our primary challenge in choosing toys for our children. Let's choose toys that develop their creativity!

Creativity isn't something a person is born with, nor is it a factor of intelligence. Any child can be taught to think more creatively. The real key to developing creativity lies in giving children choices. These choices need not be ones of quantity. They must, however, be choices that a child can make, and that a child can manipulate. A choice can be something as simple as giving a child a pad of paper and pile of crayons or colored markers and saying, "You can draw anything you choose to draw."

Finally, we as parents can choose to buy toys from companies known for their quality. No doubt there are many such companies. These are my personal favorites:

- Little Tikes (owned by Rubbermaid)
- "Toys to Grow On," a toy catalog with good toy alternatives (Long Beach, Calif.)
- "Childcraft," another quality catalog of children's toys and games (Edison, N.J.)
- Constructive Playthings (Grandview, Mo.)
- Community Playthings (Refton, N.Y.)

Many prosocial toys are produced by toy makers such as Rainfall Toys and Jonathan and David (the creators of the Precious Moments characters).

Chapter Twelve

At the Arcade

Children's playings are not sports and should be deemed their most serious actions.

—Montaigne

Good toys contain the building blocks of creativity. . . . A toy that comes complete leaves nothing for the child to bring to it. With a good toy you have only some materials, and they're not very specific. The child has to bring his creativity, his own ideas to the material, be an active participant, not just a spectator in play.

—Ruth Roufberg,
toy expert for
Children magazine

When children grow weary of cartoons and plastic toys, they move on to the electronic game fields of Nintendo, Sega, and other video game producers, where the violence continues in the form of more battles to be won.

Total sales for video games and game players topped $3.4 billion worldwide in 1989, and the market continues to escalate. Americans spent almost $600 million on entertainment programs such as interactive videos and electronic games, and that figure was expected to top $710 million in 1990. Adventure, fantasy, and science-fiction games dominate the market. It is a world that has close ties with the programs aired during Saturday morning and after-school time slots.

Sega and Atari are popular brands in the marketplace, but Nintendo continues to be the big name. It has sold more than twenty million of its entertainment systems and, this year alone, will sell more than $50 million worth of game cartridges in the U.S. Some games are so realistic they have impressed former fighter pilots.

Many video games are rooted in violence, often blowing up objects and the human beings in them. Some newer games actually portray human beings attacking other humans, complete with bloodshed.

The Nintendo player tends to be a boy between the ages of eight and fifteen, the very age when boys are most susceptible to the influence of violence in other forms of media.

The methods used on these games to exhibit violence are anything but conventional. Maces and swords are popular weapons, and bludgeoning is a common technique. One game titled Renegade has as its goal the slaughter of a gang of muggers before they toss you onto the subway tracks.

If you win at the game Double Dragon, you'll have a body count of at least fifty people and the final victim will be the hero's brother, murdered to avenge the fact that he had stolen the hero's girlfriend. Up until that point you are using an array of martial arts to fight the mysterious Shadow Boss.

The Nintendo game Life Force has the goal of destroying a reptilian creature named Zelos. The package reads, "You've gotta soar through his guts, blast past his death traps and ultimately blow out his heart."

Video games such as Nintendo's Wizard & Warriors are permeated with the occult. In Wizards & Warriors the player will encounter dungeons, levitation, potions, magical swords, and demonic warriors.

A newer role-playing game is Dragon Warrior, in which a child can call up a series of spells, initiate either a talk or a fight mode, and use a wide array of weapons. And the goal? Rescue the princess and defeat the dragon lord.

Computer games commonly are promoted on Saturday morning television programs. Saturday Supercade, for example, includes "Donkey Kong," "Donkey Kong Jr. and Uncle Pitfall," and "Pac Man." All of these are video game superstars, and their game versions are promoted in conjunction with the show.

In "The Legend of Zelda," the player encounters a demonic Pegasus, an evil character riding a unicorn, demonic winged creatures, and numerous evil spirits. This is another program based on a Nintendo game.

Movies may also relate to the games. Many children noticed that part of the music in the Turtles' movie was taken from a video game titled Ninja Gaiden. Fairly recent video games have been based on

Indiana Jones movies, as well as on *Batman, Ghostbusters II,* and *Star Trek V.*

Video games actually vary little from TV in their play value. They are solitary games. They evoke the same brain chemistry as TV. The only difference is their interaction capability, but even then the interaction between the child and the machine is rooted in violence.

At least one educator devoted a doctoral dissertation to Nintendo and concluded that the games are beneficial in that they promote certain logic and reasoning skills, and a certain amount of eye-hand coordination—if the games aren't played more than three hours a day. After that amount of time, eyestrain is possible.

Our contention is that children can develop reasoning skills and eye-hand coordination much more efficiently through other ways of playing. Putting together puzzles and building with Lego sets can develop the same skills in a lot less time with a lot more reward and fun, and generally the child can play with others at the same time.

The only socialization effects resulting from video games is that they are a common topic about which children can talk.

A troubling aspect of these games is that they can set up a child for other role-playing games as a teen. The child has already learned all of the signs and rituals from the cartoons, toys, and video games. He's ready for an even more real stage.

The game Sun Signs and Witch Hazel is considered an adult game, for ages fourteen and older, and is marketed to "those interested in astrology, magic, fortune telling, and ancient mysteries." The game has a reference booklet, a game board, eight decks of cards, twelve zodiacal medallions, thirteen amulets, three charm bags, and fifty astral projection charts, among other things. That's a lot of occult paraphernalia.

The Willow Game, based on the movie *Willow,* is a fantasy role-playing game in which each player adopts the identity of a character in the movie, becoming a part of the group who strives to carry the baby to safety or the group who wants to capture the baby and deliver it to the evil sorceress. At the heart of the play are 144 cards that set up the various moves. The game is for children eleven and older.

These games, however, are mild compared to Dungeons & Dragons, a role-playing game that has a spiritual component and has the goal of gaining spiritual power. The game is heavily based in Satan worship, demonology, witchcraft, voodoo, murder, rape, insanity, suicide, assassination, cannibalism, necromancy, and human sacrifice.

In Dungeons & Dragons, a player rolls a three- or six-sided die six times to get his six character qualities. A Dungeon Master then leads the game, using a book of plays and spells called a *Player's Handbook.* A player is asked to focus on the images in the handbook and to act in a way congruent with the character qualities he has adopted.

The role-playing is actually a sugar-coated form of psychodrama, which has been used in therapy models as a means of altering one's values and in totalitarian countries to teach children to hold values other than those taught by their parents. Players who engage in psychodramatic role-playing in Dungeons & Dragons actually adopt a full identity and all the values of that identity so that they no longer act like themselves playing a part but, indeed, as someone or something else.

Gali Sanchez, a former employee of TSI Industries, the company that manufactures Dungeons & Dragons, told Christian Broadcasting Network's reporter Steve McPheeters that he was shocked when he first read the names of the demons and devils that were going to be a part of TSI's *Monster Manual Two.* He said,

> I found that these things—names—appeared in the Bible. Moloch, where the children were taken to be sacrificed, appears in a fantasy game for kids? . . . There were names that just kept appearing and coming up, and this was not fantasy.

Sanchez's contention to his superiors at TSI was that if the game and program were truly to be fantasy, they shouldn't include authentic occult material. Although he suggested make-believe magic and made-up names, those at TSI retained the genuine occult symbols.

The Dungeons & Dragons game is constantly being updated, for further financial benefit, naturally. It continues to challenge players to explore the dark side of life.

So What's a Parent to Do?

Play your child's video games. Play long enough so you can advance through several levels, otherwise you'll miss a lot of the images that your computer-savvy child will see. Monitor them for violence and occult images.

Rent Nintendo games before you buy them, and check them before you let your child play with them.

Make a decision that you will not purchase occult or violent games! Choose, instead, educational video games that have no violence or role-playing games laced with the occult. They are available. You'll have to hunt for them, but you can find them.

Discuss the dangers of role-playing games with your child and, in greater detail, with your teenager. Don't allow the games to be played in your home, and give reasons why not. Prepare your child in advance for the possible encounter with these games at a friend's home.

Encourage your child to develop real computer skills rather than game skills. And above all, encourage your child to play without a machine as much as possible. Place emphasis on playing with friends, making things, exploring and experimenting with the real world. Encourage your child to spend time with something that is capable of talking back!

Chapter Thirteen

Browsing the Cartoon-illustrated Bookshelf

I am the master of the shadows . . . and I claim this church as my own. I smell blood, the blood of the Lamb. He's here. DRIVE HIM OUT!

—*The Gargoyle* comic book
Marvel Comics

Most parents would be shocked to know their children were reading a statement such as the one at the beginning of this chapter. Most children would consider it tame stuff.

Similar to cartoons in that they are both illustrated and rooted in action, the comic book, from a child's standpoint, is the next best thing to an animated TV show.

The concept of cartoon-illustrated printed materials is introduced early to children in today's marketplace. Masters of the Universe puts out a preschoolers series called read-alongs, that include tapes. The child is instructed to turn the page at the sound of a beep. One book tells how Eternia is protected by He-Man, who guards his world from a "demon of unimaginable evil," the wicked Skeletor. The books are presented with black-and-white illustrations, suitable for coloring, which only further involves play action with both characters and plot line.

The Care Bears, and other cartoon figures, are also featured in read-along books, cassette tapes, and illustrated books.

And then the child graduates to comic books.

The commercial comic book industry is dominated by two companies: DC Comics Inc. and Marvel Comics Group. Both can trace their roots to the earliest days of comic books, and both are now owned by larger corporations: New World Pictures owns Marvel, and Warner Communications owns DC.

Each company publishes forty to fifty titles per month, almost all devoted to superheroes. Marvel's line-up includes Spider-Man,

X-Men, Fantastic Four, and the Incredible Hulk. DC has the corner on Superman, Batman, Wonder Woman, and Teen Titans.

DC led the industry from 1937 until the late 1960s, when Marvel took the lead and turned it into a big lead. In the past few years, DC has started to catch up, largely through distribution directly to subscribers. Until the late 1970s, virtually all comic books were sold on newsstands or at local drugstores or convenience stores. Now, a large percentage is sold by direct mail.

Several independent companies are also in the marketplace—First, Comico, Eclipse, and others—and are gaining more ground by publishing what would have been considered adult-oriented material only a few years ago.

The comics are, to a great extent, the forerunners of the cartoon industry, which makes them scary from a societal and child-development standpoint. Not only are many now filled with violence, and occult and sexual activity, but if history gives a hint as to the future, these raw, vicious, and occult comic books could well be the fare on TV shortly after the turn of the century. Comic books have tended to be ten to fifteen years ahead of animated series on TV. One shudders to think what might be on the way.

In the 1960s, *Zap Comix* hit the stands. It took on religion, sexual mores, and social associations, with no topic held sacred and no innuendo unmade. It started a new era in comic books, certainly one that has redefined the word *comic.*

Actually, comic books today are perhaps best described as illustrated stories. Little in them would make one smile. To be sure, the Walt Disney titles and *Archie* are still around. But costumed characters, superheroes, and monsters are the rule.

Many comic books have viciously anti-Christian themes and plots. Some blatantly present reincarnation, spirit channeling, and the use of psychic powers and even crystals as means of gaining and exercising power.

Marvel Comic's *The Gargoyle* is obvious in its opposition to Christianity; new age heroes battle an evil force: the Christian church. Other titles exalt the religious practices of the Druids as superior to those of Christianity. Many point to Eastern gurus as the best source of wisdom and power. Others mix Christian symbols with satanic ones.

Nearly all comic books today present a universe in which there is no supreme being; there are many gods, some good and some bad. Neopaganism is at the core.

In the *Burning Hand* comic book, Jesus is actually crucified on a pentagram. One can only imagine what an animation of that plot line might look like in the year 2010.

Many comic books take on religious issues with a cynical view, such as *Binky Brown Meets the Holy Virgin Mary.* Others have been paid for by cults, such as *Brought to Light,* which was sponsored by the Christic Institute.

Justin Green, a comic book author, said this about Christianity during an interview:

> It's a myth, and yet orthodox Christians claim it's more than a myth, that it's an actuality, an historical fact. I guess I can't buy that. . . . I believe in Man.

Comic book titles today explore the world of drugs, such as the one titled *My First Acid Trip,* which is about LSD and describes the experience as joyous and transcendent.

A number of the new comic books are overtly sexual in their plots, such as *Young Lust,* as well as in their illustrations, which might make even seasoned readers of *Playboy* blush. *Elektra: Assassin* is perhaps the landmark comic of the overtly sexual genre. Gay Comix is a series of comic books advocating the homosexual lifestyle.

And what of the child fascinated with a magazine that has the Teenage Mutant Ninja Turtle characters on the cover, only to find inside a seven-page ad for a series of posters long on sorcery, images of wizards, unicorns, and the nude-from-the-waist-up image of a beautiful teenage girl.

Previews is a publication that gives information about newly released comic books. If parents picked up the February 1990 issue, for example, they'd find information about the following:

- *She-Cat #3:* "After her battle with the police, She-Cat encounters the Black Mantis, the ninja assassin who framed her for murder."

- Comic books that are adaptations of the *Teenage Mutant Ninja Turtles* movie.
- *Baker Street Children of the Night,* a mystery that takes place "when the cobblestone streets ran red with the insanity of murder."
- *Roachmill #9,* featuring a "new girl in Roachmill's life—a Play-boy centerfold no less! . . . Her 'turn-ons' include destroying buildings with a single swipe, slaughtering hapless civilians, wreaking general havoc—and eating her boyfriends."

Those are just a few titles among hundreds of similar ilk. It isn't Lulu and Jughead anymore!

The trend is increasingly toward the bizarre, the sacrilegious, and the titillating. The general style of writing and the surrealistic art of many of the books tend to advocate the weirder the better. In fact, one series of comics was called *Weirdo.*

Of one thing you can be certain: children are reading these comic books, and some of those children are going to be the TV producers of tomorrow. Warren Beatty, who produced, directed, and starred in *Dick Tracy,* admits to having been fascinated with the comic strip of Dick Tracy when he was five years old.

The hope can only be that most of what is on the comic book shelves today never sees animation, or even a second press run!

So What's a Parent to Do?

Buy your young child illustrated books that aren't linked to a TV series or movie, unless it's a series you have already prescreened for occult and violent content. Even then, skim through the book to check out the content.

Read books, not comic books, to your young children. Buy books for your children of school age so they might read them to you or read them for themselves.

Stay away from comic-book stores.

Chapter Fourteen

Let's Go to the Movies

We confess that we have sinned against you in thought, word, and deed, by what we have done . . . and by what we have left undone.

—*The Book of Common Prayer*, 1979

Parents today would be wise to play their own version of Name that Movie.

For example: Which movie features the incineration of a young boy, and the near incineration of a bosomy blonde who screams as she is lowered into a volcano; has an ample stock of whips, chains, knives, and potions; and features body parts, child slaves, spiders, voodoo dolls, magic rocks, and blood drinking? The movie was rated PG, indicating that the film industry considered it acceptable fare for children eight and older.

Which movie told the story of a life-term prisoner who was given his freedom and then single-handedly kills about a hundred enemy soldiers in a sequence of action scenes that include burning, carving, impaling, gutting, garroting, bludgeoning, exploding, hanging, and plummeting human beings? The film was rated R but has been one of the most widely rented videos by young teens.

Which movie depicts a man and a woman who become demon possessed and have sex on an altar as an act of worship to a goddess, the altar rising up from a pyramid?

Try *Indiana Jones and the Temple of Doom, Rambo: First Blood II,* and *Ghostbusters.*

What do movies have to do with Saturday morning cartoons? Actually, a great deal!

Many popular movies have and are spinning off animated series, which in turn creates a demand in children to see the movies on which the series are based. In some cases, the movies are more violent or occult than the series; in others, the cartoons are more violent. Either way, a reinforcing cycle has been strongly established between the big screen and The Box.

In the case of the Care Bears, the movie version was far more occult than the animated series. In *Care Bears Movie II,* an evil spirit occupies the body of a fourteen-year-old boy. *Rainbow Brite and the Star Stealer* was a children's movie with almost everything in it that a parent doesn't want to teach children: greed, self-centeredness, violence, sexism, and all-around evil.

The *Gremlins* movie, and animated series, is filled with nasty, mean creatures who spread a path of destruction, chaos, and death. The word *gremlin* stems from the Old English word *gemian,* meaning "to vex." *Webster's Dictionary* defines the word as "demon, evil spirit, a person or thing regarded as evil, cruel."

The movie version of *Teenage Mutant Ninja Turtles* has 194 individual acts of violence, making it far more violent than *Batman.* More than a third of the movie is devoted to fight scenes; one fight scene lasts eight minutes. But that's what ninjas do. They are warriors trained to fight.

When asked about the violence, some children interviewed said, "It was violent but not bad violent. It didn't show any blood. Just people knocking each other down."

"Rambo" and "Chuck Norris Karate Commando" cartoons turned violent R–rated movies into children's entertainment. What child didn't want to see the next Rambo or Chuck Norris movie as a result?

Robocop was another R–rated movie that became an animated series for children. According to its director, the movie version of *Robocops* had to be reedited several times just to get an R rating.

Verhoeven's most recent film, *Total Recall,* also has an R rating, but the director believes children as young as eight or nine should be allowed to see it. *Total Recall* has two hundred acts of violence, making it one of the most violent movies ever made for general release. Said Paul Verhoeven in a *USA TODAY* interview:

> We took certain things completely out, such as some of the gory parts when a dwarf hooker slices a bad guy's belly and when Arnie uses a dead body as a bullet shield, and insisted some things be left in —like when Arnie is left holding what remains of a villain's bloody arms after an elevator accident.

Ratings on movies, however, really exist only as a guide to parents. No theater is legally required to enforce the rules. As a result, many children are attending R–rated movies after their parents drop them off at theater curbsides.

Parents raised in the 1950s and early 1960s are often oblivious to this practice in their own children. They remember the days when the Saturday afternoon theater was a place for a couple of hours of hilarious misadventure, heroism, and adventure in the great outdoors, and stories of love, romance, and brave pets warmed the heart. Today's child is watching a far different screen.

Movies also have had increasingly occult themes in recent years.

Willow is the story of a child born with a mark on her arm, indicating that she is the child who could cause the downfall of the evil Queen Bavmorda and restore reign to the good people, the Daikinis. The wicked Queen's goal is to destroy the baby through the power of her magic.

On the other side of the forest, Willow Ufgood has always wanted to be a wizard. In the final battle between good and evil, a white witch helps him retrieve an occult book and grants him the power to become a wizard. After a fierce battle the evil witch's soul is sent into oblivion.

Overall, the story can be viewed as a fairly loose take-off on the story of the baby Moses in the Old Testament of the Bible. The baby in *Willow* is born with a destiny and is rescued by a midwife who runs away from the evil sorceress for as long as she can; then she places the child on a raft and floats her down the river to the place where she is found by Willow.

The emphasis in the movie is on the difference between black and white witchcraft, white witchcraft being portrayed as a good occupation to pursue.

The 1987 My Little Pony movie titled *The End of Flutter Valley* presents a message that a person must have courage. He must keep trying and test himself to the utmost. The movie draws the conclusion that Pony magic is the best magic and states, "With our kind of magic, who knows how far you'll go." The belief is strongly portrayed that from the sun come fun, laughter, happiness, hope, and song. The movie, 95 minutes of occult and religious symbols and rituals, was sponsored by Hasbro toys and Golden Books.

It's difficult for parents to see beyond some of the big-name stars who align themselves with cartoons such as "My Little Pony." What parent is going to believe that Danny DeVito, Madeline Kahn, Cloris Leachman, Rhea Perlman, and Tony Randall are going to team up to do children harm?

In 1977, Americans were blasted into hyperspace with the debut of *Star Wars*. The Star Wars trilogy—*Star Wars, Return of the Jedi,* and *The Empire Strikes Back*—has brought to the big screen almost every alien imaginable.

The movies have a strong message of the individual's responsibility to save his world through hard work, self-sacrifice, loyal friendship, and a commitment to a higher purpose. All these things, however, are accomplished in and by the individual. Courage is the supreme characteristic.

Whatever creator George Lucas's intended message, the movies are filled with strong symbols related to the occult.

Darth Vader, the focus for evil in the series, is modeled in a way that shows strong similarities to the Nordic god Oden.

In *The Empire Strikes Back,* viewers will encounter Yoda, an extraterrestrial, who has been referred to as a Zen master by the director of the movie, Irvin Kershner, who is a self-admitted Zen Buddhist. Texe Marrs, in the book *Ravaged by the New Age,* cites the presence of a demon named Mephistopheles in a 1928 book titled *Secret Teachings of All Ages.* The character therein, who appears magically on the spot at which a pentagram has been drawn, bears a remarkable resemblance to Yoda. But Americans at large have seen little danger in the Yoda character, making him all the more a deception, a demonic creature at work under the guise of goodness and truth.

The Star Wars trilogy paved the way for another blockbuster movie with occult overtones: *E.T.—The Extraterrestrial.*

In *E.T.,* viewers see:

- children playing Dungeons & Dragons in the opening scene
- examples of mental telepathy between E.T. and his host child after E.T. drinks beer
- a characterization of E.T. that bears strong parallels (from a rather dark side) to the life of Jesus Christ

E.T. came from the heavenlies and possesses superhuman knowledge and power. He appears in rather humble surroundings. He communes with a fairly select group of children, performs healings, and keeps trying to contact his captain. He defies natural laws, including gravity, and is melancholy as he is dying. He dies, of course, to save Elliott, and is resurrected from the dead by the captain. He is ultimately taken up by the spaceship to be with the captain and crew and tells Elliott that he'll always be with him in his heart.

I recently had a conversation with one screenwriter of *E.T.*, a man deeply troubled at his involvement with the movie. He told me about the visual subliminals the screenwriters wove into the movie, many of which were specifically designed to enhance the reputation of and change the nation's thinking about the homosexual community.

Said Steven Spielberg, the movie's creator, about E.T. in an interview reported in *The Best of Starlog:*

> There was severe reverence on the set shown by everybody, even the guys who swept the floors, toward E.T. Severe reverence. . . . [The kids] believed in E.T. the way we believe in Santa Claus . . . or should believe in Santa Claus. Everybody had such a belief in E.T. as a living, breathing organism that no one would dare go up to him and make fun of his appearance or make fun of his awkwardness. He really did seem to have a life of his own.

Even the Disney movies aren't immune to overtones of darkness and the occult.

Consider the entire plot line of the Disney release *Escape to Witch Mountain.* An orphaned boy and girl have abundant psychic powers in this tale. They use levitation techniques throughout the movie. Both children possess and portray other psychic abilities that allow them to do such things as foretell the future, tame a horse, and control a guard dog.

All is considered to be okay with these children, however, because in the final minutes of the movie, the audience is told that the children are really from another planet and were stranded on earth when their spacecraft malfunctioned.

Or what about the Disney release of *Howard the Duck?* Howard the

Duck lives on a planet that is a twin of earth where ducks, rather than apes, have supposedly evolved into the most intelligent life form. An energy inversion captures him and transports him to Cleveland, Ohio, where he gets a job at a massage parlor. Ultimately he develops a friendship and love interest in the female leader of a rock band. But the worst is still to come. The head of the science project that inadvertently brought Howard to earth becomes demon possessed when he attempts to help Howard get back home.

Disney cartoons often have a dark side that goes unnoticed because many of the stories are familiar fairy tales.

Consider, for example, the commemorative videotape of Walt Disney mini-classics called *Mickey's Magical World.* The theme of the video reinforces much of what a child sees on Saturday morning television: magic is all around us. The video teaches that determination results in magic, imagination is a key for magic, and practice makes better magic.

A number of Disney feature cartoons are steeped in occult figures and activities, including *Sleeping Beauty, Snow White, Fantasia,* and *Bedknobs and Broomsticks.* Parents often get lost in the beautiful animation of Disney movies and the gags that cause children and adults alike to smile, and they fail to see the overall message of many of these tales.

Early predictions that the growing video industry would destroy theater business haven't held true. The two complement each other.

Many videos available for rental fall into the classification of "scarytales." About one-fourth of the $1.6 billion that Americans spend each year to rent videos is spent on these horror and suspense films.

I was shocked the first time I went to rent horror videos as part of the research for my book *Horror and Violence.* Each time I went to the video store I was able to get only one or two movies, even on weekdays, because they were all rented.

One psychiatrist actually uses slasher films to help his clients. Dr. Jeffrey Turley, a child psychiatrist and fellow at the University of Virginia, rented the video of *Friday the 13th* to use in a therapy session with a fourteen-year-old boy who axed the interior of his family's home.

Said Dr. Turley in an interview with a reporter from the *Dallas Morning News,* "He [the boy] wasn't sure why he had done it, but he felt he was addicted to slasher movies. . . . We watch fifteen minutes of the film, stop it at some point, and I ask him to explain his thoughts and motives."

Dr. Turley finds that the teenagers he encounters have fears about the world at large and see the world generally as a dangerous place. He believes the movies speak to teenagers about their feelings of vulnerability. (As discussed earlier, those feelings may have been evoked, in part, through their experience with The Box!)

An attempt to confront fear and thereby overcome it may be one reason children rent horror films in the first place. In many slasher films, such as *Nightmare on Elm Street, Halloween,* and *Friday the 13th,* a teenager is able to survive the random slaughter of his friends and summon the power to overcome the evil aggressor. What hasn't been determined, however, is why children and teens seem to feel compelled to watch these movies again and again.

In a recent survey, we found that the average ten- to thirteen-year-old presently is watching one hundred R–rated movies a year. These are movies that a child is supposedly restricted from seeing in a theater until he is seventeen years old. But children rent them at video stores, often without their parents' knowledge.

What do most of these R–rated movies have as a theme? Horror and violence. The children aren't seeking out sexual movies nearly as much as the fright-at-night movies.

When parents today think of horror movies, they often refer to their childhood experiences with *Dracula, Frankenstein, The Blob,* or *Invasion of the Body Snatchers.*

We're talking about a completely different ballgame today.

One out of six movies released from Hollywood last year had a violent rape scene. Not just rape, which is an act of violence in itself, but rape and murder, rape and decapitation, rape and mutilation, rape and torture, and so forth.

Children today see sexual scenes linked to violence even before they have had a chance to have a decent, normal, hand-holding relationship of their own with the opposite sex. They see sex and violence in the most graphically portrayed manner, often linked with humor. How can their emotional systems be anything but skewed?

"But my children have never been allowed to see such trash," you may say.

Are you sure?

Most children don't see these videos in their own homes. Some see them at slumber parties and when they stay with friends. Others watch them with their friends in the playrooms or in the upstairs bedrooms of their friends' homes while parents are away or are watching other programs downstairs on the family's main TV set.

Still others are picked up at the local theater, where a little theater hopping happens and where management frequently decides to turn the other way and let youngsters of all ages watch what they will.

Parents also need to be aware that some videos are released unrated. Segments that might have been cut, even from an X–rated movie, are often put back into the video-release version.

Consider some of the newer titles making the young teen scene. *Assault of the Killer Bimbos* features five tough women outfitted in mini-, studded leather skirts and bra-less tank tops. Or how about *Curse of the Cannibal Confederates, Bloodsucking Freaks, Screamplay, Zombie Island Massacre, Chainsaw Hookers, Class of Nuke 'Em High,* or *Space Sluts in the Slammer?* David Hutchings and Doug Lindeman, in writing for *People* magazine, call this genre grade Z movies.

One of the most popular videos of the slash-and-gash genre is *The Faces of Death.* This film is devoted to showing clear depictions of people dying violently, and 80 percent of the film is taken from newsreels, film libraries, and home movies. The scenes include a shark tearing apart a skin diver; a man setting himself on fire; assassinations; pit bull fights; snake handlers; a suicide leap; three drowning victims; a man who is mauled by a grizzly bear; footage from the Jewish holocaust during World War II; the aftermath of a private airplane crash; and so forth. The movie is one of the worst viewing experiences of my life. This video has been banned in forty-six nations, but more than 160,000 copies are still circulating in the United States.

Among the scenes a child can see by watching the popular horror film *Faces of Death* are the following:

- A restaurant scene in which a waiter serves a live monkey to two patrons and provides them with small hammers so that they can crack open the monkey's skull and eat its brains.

- A gunfight in Los Angeles where the camera follows policemen into a house where they find a woman who has had her throat sliced open.

- A real-life cult murder in which the corpse is shown lying on a pentagram, the body is cut open, and the organs are eaten and the blood smeared on the participants in the rite.

Children who watch such horror movies appear to become addicted to their own adrenaline. Fear produces a chemical response that acts as a high.

Often when I tell about these movies, parents shudder that teenagers are seeing such garbage. They are shocked when I explain that it's not only teens who are watching.

A group of ten- and eleven-year-olds who had seen the movie *Friday the 13th* were asked to tell their favorite moments from the movie. One child wrote, "I liked the part where the girl chopped off her dad's head and ate it as a birthday cake."

One video store owner in a fairly rural area told me recently that a five-year-old girl had come into his store and requested a movie she had already seen. She couldn't recall the title, but she repeated some of the dialogue. The movie was *Nightmare on Elm Street.* The man told me he made a decision that night to pull all R–rated videos from his shelves.

The video rentals of the *Nightmare on Elm Street* series topped $7 billion in 1989. In spite of several legislative moves at the state level (most notably, Missouri), video stores can rent these videos, and others like them, to any person of any age.

So What's a Parent to Do?

Take your child to see only those PG–rated movies that you have already seen and of which you approve. Never take your child or young teen to see an R–rated movie.

Talk to the parents of your child's friends. Discuss the proliferation of horror videos circulating among teens. Map out a game plan that will allow you to take a group stand against these videos. Then discuss your policy with your teens. Talk about why you don't want your child watching this garbage.

Control your own VCR. Know what's being played on it and when.

Parents need to gain confidence that they can control what is brought into the safety and comfort of their own homes to keep those homes safe and comfortable. Parents can say no to the media. They can say no to visual images and audio messages that they don't want played in their own homes. They have that authority and that responsibility.

Sadly, too many parents seem to think they can't govern their households without alienating their children. They can. And if they need help learning how to do it, it is better to get that professional advice through individual or family counseling than to allow a child to fill his mind with harmful images and messages.

Chapter Fifteen

What Next?

I take the trash out twice a week to be collected by the garbage man. But with television, it is increasingly a case of bringing the trash into the house seven days and nights a week. It has so much garbage on it that it might violate clean air standards of the Environmental Protection Agency.

—Radio commentator **Cal Thomas**
June 27, 1985

Saturday morning cartoons

Plus weekday syndicated programs

Plus the violence and sexual images of prime-time and daytime TV

Plus toys and games

Plus video games, role-playing games, Saturday afternoon television, movies, videos.

They all add up.

The overall effect is one I term layer upon layer. The Bible describes this cumulative training in this way: line upon line, precept upon precept, here a little, there a little (see Isa. 28:10).

And the trend toward the future points only toward more consumption of a more graphic and more potent set of visual cues and more extensive cross marketing of products.

What might we expect in the future of children's TV?

First, very high density television (VHDTV) is only a matter of years away. The image with VHDTV is extremely sharp, making any scene all that much more realistic.

Second, holographic TV seems to be more than just a wish of researchers. Holographic viewing, which gives three-dimensional viewing, would give the ultimate in realism.

Third, fiber-optic cable networks and mini-satellite dishes, some of which are envisioned to embed invisibly in an average-size window or skylight, will multiply viewing options. As many as 160 channels will soon be available to viewers.

It's not absurd to project that by the year 2000, most people in the U.S. will have upwards of 200 channels available to them for their viewing choices. With the advent of smaller dishes connecting viewers at home directly to satellites, the cable systems of today may even go the way of yesterday's rooftop antennas.

Virtually all these methods will bear an enhanced capacity to teach our children—with greater quantity of material available, greater clarity of image, greater detail and realism, but without any guarantees that the content of television's message will have any greater quality.

I've even read one think piece recently that suggests a viewer's brain waves may one day be interactive with TV. Information would be caught, not taught.

Of one thing we can be fairly certain: Americans will continue to watch TV.

According to the Bureau of Social Research in Washington, D.C., nearly two-thirds of Americans are watching TV on any given winter evening, other than a major holiday such as Christmas or New Year's Eve. Of the remaining one-third, most are not watching TV because they are obligated to be engaged in another activity, such as working on a night shift, attending choir practice at church, working late, and so forth. Less than 10 percent of the population chooses not to watch TV on an average winter's night.

It is still possible to turn off the TV. However, it is no longer possible to turn off the total TV environment.

We Americans are getting our primal impressions about life from a machine. The period since 1950 is the first time in history that children will hear more stories from a machine than from an adult. What this innovation might mean for the development of the human consciousness twenty or fifty years from now, nobody knows.

We as adults, however, have two inescapable responsibilities for all children in our society: (1) to protect them and (2) to provide opportunities for them to grow and mature. Fulfilling these responsibilities doesn't mean that we shield children from everything that may be considered bad in the world. It does mean that when we give our children images and words and model behavior for them, we are responsible as adults to tell them the meaning behind those images, words, and behavior. We have the responsibility for conveying the truth and an adequate representation of reality as we know it to be.

One must ask then, Is it bad for children to watch today's TV programs? Are those programs detrimental to their physical, mental, emotional, and spiritual growth?

We must also ask, Are we teaching on TV what we want our children to learn so they might lead our culture into the next generation? Does TV give them a true picture of the world?

Most of what we have presented in this book leads us to answer the first two questions yes and the next two questions no.

So What's a Parent to Do?

A parent can limit TV viewing time.

Parents are generally perceived to be the controllers of the TV set(s) in their home. From our observation and study of parents and children, that simply isn't the case.

Often a child decides what is going to be watched on the main set, with parents showing an amazing willingness to trust a child's judgment about what is fun or good to watch.

And what about the second, or third, or fourth TV set? If Mom or Dad wants to watch the nightly news at 5:30, Junior can opt for "He-Man and Masters of the Universe" on his own set upstairs!

Parents can begin limiting TV viewing by making some strict rules that no TV will be watched before school, during meals, or before homework is completed. That rule alone would eliminate many programs on weekday afternoons that are occult-based and extremely violent.

We also suggest that you make a no-TV rule for designated nights of the week. Make those family times instead. You might call them exploring days or activity days.

You might consider requiring that a child spend at least half an hour reading and at least half an hour in free-form play by himself or with friends for every half hour of TV viewing.

Above all, avoid programs with violence, horror, sexual content, or occult symbols and activity.

"But how can I tell in advance?" you may ask.

Only one sure-fire way exists: watch it yourself. We heartily recommend that you tape programs and play them later for your child.

Granted, that takes extra effort; nobody ever said teaching a child was easy or automatic.

For preschoolers, we recommend that they not be allowed to watch more than thirty minutes of TV a day.

Rather than go cold turkey with these new habits, you may want first to keep a family TV log of your present viewing habits. Then spend another week or so rating the various programs. Talk about TV and the viewing habits in your home, especially if you have elementary-aged children or teenagers. Let your children come to the conclusion with you that they are watching a great deal of TV, and that many of the programs they are presently viewing aren't even all that pleasurable to watch.

You may want to make the switch to a monitor-only system for the TV set that your child watches. In other words, use a unit that plays videotapes but does not receive broadcast or cable programs.

Plan what you and your children are going to watch on TV.

Don't turn on the TV at random. Make it a deliberate act to watch something you've already determined that you want to see. You may want to allow your child to select one or two programs from a prescreened list you have made.

Set a viewing time limit for each day. Let your child see that choices have to be made among programs, in the same way that choices are made throughout life about how a person is going to spend his or her time.

Encourage watching a wide range of programs.

Talk about your TV viewing choices with your child. If a child questions your decision about a program, explain why you do or do not like it. When a program coincides with your family's viewpoints or value structure, tell your child why. Give your child the opportunity to help choose activities other than watching TV.

One method used by some parents is called a TV contract. Each child, for example, may be allowed to choose five hours of TV per week from programs that have parental preapproval. Some parents don't allow their children to rechoose or to make up programs that might be missed once the schedule is made (assuming that the child has chosen other activities instead of the program). Some parents insist that at least three programs have to be educational or cultural.

Recognize that some shows are simply better turned off or

avoided. The following list is my evaluation of today's key programs.

Cartoons to turn off because they portray sex, violence, and the occult.

"Aquaman"
"Centurions"
"Challenge of the Go-Bots"
"Defenders of the Earth"
"Dungeons and Dragons"
"G.I. Joe"
"He-Man and Masters of the Universe"
"Inhumanoids"
"Jayce and the Wheeled Warriors"

"Jem"
"Kidd Video"
"Kissyfur"
"MASK"
"Rainbow Brite"
"Robotech"
"She-Ra—Princess of Power"
"Silverhawks"
"Transformers"
"Voltron"

The following often use occult symbols, mystical experiences, and criminal activities. Use caution.

"Alvin and the Chipmunks"
"Aquaman"
"Batman"
"Care Bears"
"Casper"
"Droids and Ewoks"
"Gummie Bears"
"Hulk Hogan Rock 'n' Wrestling"
"Mighty Mouse"

"Muppet Show/Muppet Babies"
"Punky Brewster"
"Richie Rich"
"Speed Racer"
"Superman"
"Superpowers"
"Teen Wolf"
"Wonder Woman"

These are programs we regard as acceptable.

"Berenstain Bears"
"Davey and Goliath"
"Fat Albert and the Cosby Kids"

"Glo Friends"
"Popples"
"Potato Head Kids"
"Foofur"

"The Get Along Gang"   The old series of
"Rocky Raccoon"   "Winnie the Pooh"

**These are especially well-produced programs
that can aid your child's education.**

For children 2 to 5
   "Sesame Street" (PBS)
   "Welcome to Pooh Corner" (Disney)
   "Babar" (HBO)
   "You and Me, Kid" (Disney)

For children 6 to 11
   "WonderWorks" (PBS)
   "Mr. Wizard World" (Nickelodeon)
   "Square One TV" (PBS)
   "Reading Rainbow" (PBS)

**These are best watched as a family but generally
acceptable if an adult is present to discuss
some issues.**

"Nova" (PBS)
"Life Goes On" (ABC)
"ABC After School Specials" (ABC)

Watch TV with your children.

My advice to parents is to spend at least half of your child's
planned and approved viewing time watching along with her. You
might make it a game with your child. Keep a log together. Look for
racial stereotypes, violence, and occult behavior. Watch your child
watch the screen. Does your child get overly excited? Does she look
disturbed or confused? If so, talk about those scenes or segments
with your child as soon as possible after the program is over. If the
scene is disturbing enough, turn it off and talk about it immediately.

Talk about the commercials, too.

Give your child your opinions as to what you consider to be socially acceptable behavior. Tell why.

Children are constantly looking for approval, primarily from their
parents, and then from teachers, other children, and so forth. When

they see behavior on TV that appears to be more, or less, socially acceptable than they had thought, they will adjust their thinking. Your job as a parent is to monitor those adjustments and help make mid-course corrections.

Children also want to see what works. They want to see what behavior gets rewarded. When a child sees behavior rewarded on TV, he tends to adjust his behavior accordingly. Again, your job as a parent is to make sure your child is drawing the right conclusions.

Children are also sexual beings and can be sexually aroused. When children see behavior that is sexually exciting, they view it in a positive manner regardless of the context because their bodies feel pleasure. Be sensitive to this fact as you and your children watch TV together.

Be continually on guard that your child may be exposed to certain issues, behaviors, and symbols that are beyond his level of development or understanding. Be aware that his innocence may be raped by some programs.

"But what if I'm watching the news and my child walks through and sees something horrific?" Parents often ask me such questions about the violence displayed on the news.

I suggest they give the child an opportunity to talk about what he has seen, and then address the concerns. That's also a good evening to read the child an extra book or two at bedtime or to have a prolonged time of play together. Give the child a couple of extra hugs and kisses. Bear in mind that the child's sense of security has been challenged, and he needs reassurance that he is safe from scary happenings in his own home.

Be on guard as to other places and times your children will be exposed to TV programs.

If your child is going to a slumber party, or any party for that matter, or is going to sleep over at a friend's house, ask the child's parents before the party whether there is going to be videotape entertainment. If a program is going to be shown about which you have qualms, suggest an alternative to the parent.

Baby-sitters need to be given strict house rules for the use of TV. In fact, it's generally a good idea to map out the schedule you want a sitter to follow, listing activities for every half hour—game time, story time, bath and toothbrushing time, snack time, and so forth. Schedule out TV or leave an approved video for both baby-sitter and child to watch.

Recently I attended a church service in which all those aged four and under were dismissed just before the guest speaker was introduced. Where were the children going? Downstairs to watch *Cinderella!* Ask your children what they are watching at school, and even at church or synagogue, when you are occupied elsewhere. If videos are being shown to children at your place of worship, talk to your minister, priest, or rabbi about the titles being shown. If they are ones you question, give your minister a copy of this book!

Finally, when you don't like what you see on TV, say so.

Let your local station know. Let the networks know. Let the toy companies know. Let the sponsors of the program know. Let your political representatives know.

Be aware that we are exporting these programs, too. Most of what appears on prime-time in our nation is broadcast widely around the world or made available on videotapes. You may want to register some concern to your representatives and senators about exporting violent, sexual, or occult programs.

The Federal Communications Commission deregulated children's programming in 1984, but a move was made again in 1987 to reinstate the FCC guidelines limiting advertising to 9½ minutes per hour on weekend mornings and 12 minutes per hour on weekdays. A bill in Congress recently was passed limiting advertising to 11 minutes per hour on weekend mornings.

A bill was introduced in the Congressional Telecommunications Subcommittee by Congressmen Ed Markey and Terry Bruce after heavy lobbying from the Action for Children's Television group, which vigorously opposes what it calls "thirty minute commercials for toys."

ACT also filed a petition with the FCC claiming that product-based children's programs violate a long-standing FCC policy that requires a separation between programming and advertising. The FCC undertook an inquiry, but the intent of the inquiry was to determine whether toy makers should be "required to be identified as sponsors of the show" and not whether toys can be the featured performers of a program.

Specifically, ACT asked that a reasonable number of announcements be required for certain cartoon programs, stating that the program material is an attempt to promote the sale of the products shown in the story.

The move failed.

You may want to write to your representatives about these issues relating to advertising and commercial time.

The National Council of the Churches of Christ in the U.S.A. has called upon Congress and the Federal Communications Commission to study the incidences of violence in programs and to publish regularly their findings, to require that audiences be warned in advance about the level of violence and sexual content in programs, and to require that cable TV companies make readily available a means by which parents can exercise a right to prevent their children from viewing programs they deem unsuitable.

The Council has also asked Congress and the FCC to reinstate the historic process of broadcasters' regularly surveying their audiences to determine community needs and interests.

To date, no action has been taken.

You may want to write to your representatives about these issues.

Parents often take a position either of ignoring what is on TV or of accepting it. Ignoring what is on, of course, is also accepting it.

Many make an assumption that simply because it's on TV and it's for children, nothing can be wrong with it.

Many parents assume that if the cartoon doesn't show blatant drug use, beer drinking by kids, or blood, it's okay.

Don't fall into those categories.

We must bear in mind always that the total effects of TV are more likely to be long-range than immediate.

In the same way that it takes several months or years for a person to gain excess weight to the point of obesity, or for the accumulation of chemical stresses to trigger malignant cell growth, so it takes months or years of heavy TV watching for the video residue to build up in children.

Any activity that takes up so much of the time of so many people as television does must surely be taken seriously as a major influence on any society or segment of society and regarded as a primary shaper of tomorrow's world.

It's time for us as adults to confront The Box and to exert our power over it.

If we don't, it will surely continue to exert its power over us and, more important, over the Young Child that each one of us knows and loves.

Bibliography of
Key References

1. Associated Press. "Too Much TV Can Make Child Violent or Fat, Doctors Warn."

2. Auerbach, Stevanne. *The Toy Chest—A Complete Sourcebook of Toys for Children.* Secaucus, N.J.: Lyle Stuart Inc., 1986.

3. Berkowitz, L., and P. Tannenbaum. *Violence and the Media.*

4. Bettelheim, Bruno. "The Importance of Play." *Atlantic Monthly,* March 1987, pp. 35+.

5. Bohbot, Alan. "Tube Talk—A History of Kids' TV." *Toy & Hobby,* February 1988, p. 138.

6. Brown, Heidi Nolte. "Can Violent Films Help Troubled Teens?" *Dallas Morning News,* March 11, 1990.

7. Butler, Annie L., Edward Earl Gotts, and Nancy L. Quisen Gerry. *Play as Development.* New York: Charles E. Merrill Publishers, 1978.

8. Calkins, Candi. "Video Vegetation: Is TV Producing Couch Potato Kids?" *Standard* (Virginia Beach: CBN University), November-December 1988, p. 5.

9. Cantor, Muriel G., and Joel M. Cantor. "Do Soaps Teach Sex?"

10. Childers, Kim Walsh, and Jane Brown. "Teen Media Awareness Mirrors Upbringing."

11. *Child's Play—Developmental and Applied.* New York: Lawrence Earl Baum Associates Publishers, 1984.

12. Clift, Amy Alice. "The God in the Electronic Box: Children's Television and the Occult." Unpublished manuscript, December 1986.

13. Cline, Victor B., ed. *Where Do You Draw the Line?—An Exploration into Media Violence, Pornography, and Censorship.* Provo, Utah: Brigham Young University Press, 1977.

14. Cline, Victor B., Roger G. Croft, and Steven Courrier. "The Desensitization of Children to TV Violence."

15. Cohen, Dorothy. "Is TV a Pied Piper?" *Young Children Journal,* November 1974, pp. 12+.

16. Collier, James Lincoln. "What Really Scares Kids." *Marriage Partnership,* Spring 1989, pp. 100+.

17. Comstock, George. *TV and Human Behavior.* New York: Columbia University Press, 1978.

18. ————."Special Section: Television—A Hard, Long, Look." *Connoisseur,* September 1989, pp. 135+.

19. Cumbey, Constance E. *The Hidden Dangers of the Rainbow: The New Age Movement and Our Coming Age of Barbarism.* Shreveport, La.: Huntingdon House, Inc., 1983.

20. *Eerdmans Handbook of the World Religions.* Grand Rapids, Mich.: Eerdmans, 1982.

21. Endrst, James. "Getting the Kids Back—Fighting a Losing Battle Against TV for Mind of Child," syndicated column.

22. Esteves, Roland. "Children's TV: A Guide for Parents." *Marriage and Family Living,* January 1982, pp. 14+.

23. Eysenck, H. J., and D. K. B. Nias. *Sex, Violence and the Media.* New York: Maurice Temple Smith, 1980.

24. Faivelson, Saralie. "Verdict on TV Violence." *Woman's Day,* October 1, 1987, p. 24.

25. Foutz, Diana. "Who's in the Dollhouse?"

26. Garvey, Catherine. *Play.* Boston: Harvard University Press, 1977.

27. Gaynor, Frank, ed. *Dictionary of Mysticism.* New York: Citadel Press, Philosophical Library, 1958.

28. Gesell, Arnold. *The Mental Growth of the Pre-School Child.* New York: Scholarly, 1968.

29. Goldsen, Rose K. *The Show and Tell Machine—How Television Works and Works You Over.* New York: Dial Press, 1975.

30. Groth, Gary, and Robert Fiore. *The New Comics.* New York: Berkley Books, 1988.

31. Hamill, Pete. "Crack and the Box." *Esquire,* May 1990, pp. 63+.

32. Hardy, Dale D. "A Look at Cartoons." Unpublished manuscript, 1986.

33. Hathaway, Nancy. *The Unicorn.* New York: Avenel Press, 1984, p. 161.

34. ————."Let Children Feel Compassion: Curb Television Violence." *Journal News* (Rockland County, N.Y.).

35. Kantrowitz, Barbara, and Pat Wingert. "How Kids Learn." *Newsweek,* April 17, 1979, pp. 50+.

36. Kellam, Jeff. "Decoding MTV: Values, View and Videos."

37. Kosinski, Jerzy. *Television and Values.* The Learning Seed Company, March 30, 1982.

38. Lappe, Frances Moor. *What to Do After You Turn Off the TV.* New York: Ballantine Books, 1985.

39. Levinson, Richard, and William Link. *OFF CAMERA—Conversations with the Makers of Prime-Time Television.* New York: New American Library, 1986.

40. Liebert, Robert M., Emily S. Davidson, and John M. Neale. *Aggression in Childhood: The Impact of Television.*

41. Liebert, Robert M., Joyce N. Sprafkin, and Emily S. Davidson. *The Early Window—Effects of Television on Children and Youth.* New York: Pergamon Press, 1982.

42. Ludtke, Melissa. "How to Neutralize G.I. Joe." *Time,* March 26, 1990, pp. 84+.

43. Mander, Jerry. *Four Arguments for the Elimination of Television.* New York: Morrow Quill Paperbacks, 1978.

44. Marrs, Texe. *Ravaged by the New Age.* Austin, Tex.: Living Truth Publishers, 1989.

45. ———. "CBN Reports on Dungeons and Dragons," *Media Spotlight,* April–June 1986, p. 8.

46. Melody, William. *Children's Television—The Economics of Exploitation.* New Haven, Conn.: Yale University Press, 1973.

47. Miller, Susanna. *The Psychology of Play.* New York: Penguin Books, 1968.

48. ———. *Model and Toy Collection.* Seville, Ohio: Cap'n Penny Productions, 1990.

49. Morrison, Melissa. "Mixed Signals." *Dallas Morning News,* June 3, 1990.

50. Munger, Evelyn Moats, and Susan Jane Bowdon. *Child-Play—Activities for Your Child's First Three Years.* New York: Dutton, 1983.

51. Naha, Ed. "Inside E.T." *The Best of Starlog,* June 1983, pp. 18+.

52. ———. "Young Britons Told Not to Copy Batman." *New York Times,* August 25, 1966.

53. Newenhuyse, Elizabeth Cody. "Remember When You Were a Kid?" *Marriage Partnership,* Spring 1989, pp. 102+.

54. O'Connor, John J. "Cartoons Teach Children, But Is the Lesson Good?" *New York Times,* February 20, 1990.

55. ———."What Are TV Ads Selling to Children?" *Advertising Age,* July 24, 1989, p. 34.

56. Padus, Emrika. "Do War Toys Make Sense?" *Good Toys,* Fall 1986, pp. 26+.

57. Palmer, Edward L., and Aimee Dorr. *Children and the Faces of Television.* New York: Academic Press, 1980.

58. Perry, Susan. "Fear of Strangers—War Toys and Action Figures Are Stimulating Kids' Natural Aggression." *L.A. Parent Magazine,* April 1987.

59. Phillips, Phil. *Turmoil in the Toybox.* Lancaster, Pa.: Starburst Publishers, 1986.

60. Phillips, Phil, and Joan Hake Robie. *Halloween and Satanism.* Lancaster, Pa.: Starburst Publishers, 1987.

61. Phillips, Phil, and Joan Hake Robie. *Horror and Violence —The Deadly Duo in the Media.* Lancaster, Pa.: Starburst Publishers, 1988.

62. Piers, Maria, and Genevieve Millet Landau. *The Gift of Child's Play.* New York: Walker and Co., 1980.

63. Radecki, Thomas. "International Coalition Against Violent Entertainment." Press release, April 20, 1987.

64. Reader's Free for All: "Bart T-shirts Aren't Right at Schools." *Dallas Morning News,* June 3, 1990.

65. Reese, Michael. "A Mutant 'Ozzie and Harriet.' " *Newsweek,* December 15, 1989.

66. ———."Coalition on TV Violence Says War Toys Now the Most Popular." *Religious News Service,* July 16, 1985.

67. Roehlkepartain, Jolene L. "The Lure of Teenage Mutant Ninja Turtles." *Jr. High Ministry,* May–August 1989.

68. Rosemond, John. "Taming the TV Monster." *Better Homes & Gardens,* September 1988, pp. 26+.

69. Rubin, Kenneth H. "Fantasy Play: Its Role in the Development of Social Skills and Social Cognition." New Directions for Child Development #9, in *Children's Play.* San Francisco: Jossey-Bass, Inc., 1980.

70. Scarfe, Neville V. "Play: An Agent for Learning Social Values." In *Play: Children's Business,* Association for Childhood Education International.

71. Schwantes, Dave. *Taming Your TV and Other Media.* Nashville: Southern Publishing Assoc., 1981.

72. Schwartz, Marlyn. "It's High Time Barbie Faced Reality." *Dallas Morning News,* December 24, 1989.

73. Schwartzman, Helen. "The Sociocultural Context of Play." In *Play and Learning.* New York: Gardner Press, 1979.

74. Seuling, Barbara. *You Can't Show Kids in Underwear and Other Little Known Facts about Television.* New York: Doubleday, 1982, p. 82.

75. Shapiro, Laura. "Guns and Dolls." *Newsweek,* May 28, 1990, pp. 56+.

76. Siegel, Alberta. "The Effects of Media Violence on Social Learning."

77. Smith, Robin. "Television Addiction." *Perspectives on Media Effects,* Lawrence Earl Gaum Associates, 1986, pp. 109+.

78. Sobel, Robert. *The Manipulators—America in the Media Age.* New York: Anchor Press/Doubleday, 1976.

79. ———."Syndicators Unleash Flood of First-run Kid Products." *Television/Radio Age,* August 20, 1984, pp. 33+.

80. Stein, Ben. *The View from Sunset Boulevard.* New York: Basic Books, 1979.

81. ———."Toys and Even Better Play." *The Hume Moneyletter,* April 24, 1985.

82. Theisen, Earl. "The History of Cartoons." *International Photographer,* March 1933, pp. 14+.

83. ———." ACT Urges FCC to Identify Kids' Program-Length Ads." *Toy & Hobby,* April 1986.

84. ———."ACT & FCC Debate Rules on Kids' Advertising Programs." *Toy & Hobby,* November 1987, p. 10.

85. ———."Toys Today." *Playthings,* February 1990.

86. ———."How TV Influences Your Kids." *TV Guide,* March 1990, pp. 24+.

87. ———."Parent's Guide to Children's Television." *TV Guide,* March 1990, pp. 6+.

88. ———."Who Decides What Your Kids Watch." *TV Guide,* March 1990.

89. ———."Topic: Teenage Killers." *USA TODAY,* November 8, 1987.

90. Vanderkooij, Rimmert. *That's All in the Game.*

91. Wedo, Bill. "Young Critics Dissect the Appeal of 'Ninja.' " *Dallas Morning News,* April 22, 1990.

92. Wertham, Fredric. *School for Violence, Mayhem in the Mass Media.*

93. White, Mary Alice. *TC Today* (Newsletter of Teachers College Columbia University), Fall 1981.

94. White, William R. *Stories for Telling: A Treasury for Christian Storytellers.* Minneapolis: Augsburg, 1986, p. 9.

95. Wilkins, Joan Anderson. *Breaking the TV Habit.* New York: Charles Scribner's Sons.

96. Wistrick, Enid. *"I Don't Mind the Sex, It's the Violence"—Film Censorship Explored.* London: Marion Boyars.

97. Wloszczyna, Susan. "Cowabunga! USA Kids Are Totally Turtles." *USA TODAY,* March 30–April 1, 1990.

98. Workman, Diana. "What You See Is What You Think." *Media & Values,* Spring 1989, pp. 3+.

Appendix A

Addresses to Which You May Register Complaints or Support

To register a complaint about toys

Commissioner
U.S. Consumer Product Safety Commission
Washington, D.C. 20207

To register a complaint with the toy industry

Executive Director
Toy Manufacturers of America
200 Fifth Avenue
New York City, NY 10010

To register a complaint about toy advertising

Director
Children's Advertising Review
Council of Better Business Bureaus, Inc.
845 Third Avenue
New York City, NY 10022

Director
Children's Advertising
National Association of Broadcasters
477 Madison Avenue
New York City, NY 10022

To register a complaint to the networks

Programming Department
American Broadcasting Company (ABC)
1330 Avenue of the Americas
New York City, NY 10019

Programming Department
Columbia Broadcasting System (CBS)
51 West Fifty-second Street
New York City, NY 10019

Programming Department
National Broadcasting Corporation (NBC)
30 Rockefeller Plaza
New York City, NY 10020

Programming Department
Public Broadcasting Service (PBS)
485 L'Enfant Plaza West, SW
Washington, D.C. 20024

To register a complaint with the FCC

Chairman
Federal Communications Commission
1919 M. Street, NW
Washington, D.C. 20554

To register a complaint with the leading magazines that serve the toy trade

Editor
Playthings Magazine
51 Madison Avenue
New York City, NY 10010

Editor
Toy & Hobby World
1107 Broadway
New York City, NY 10010

Editor
Toy Trade News
757 Third Avenue
New York City, NY 10010

To get more information or to show your support for activities that advocate improvement of children's television

Peggy Charren
Action for Children's Television
46 Austin St.
Newtonville, MA 02160

National Citizen's Committee for Broadcasting
1028 Connecticut Ave., NW
Washington, D.C. 20036

Cult Awareness Network
P.O. Box 608370
Chicago, IL 60626
(312) 267-7777

National Coalition on Television Violence
Thomas Radecki, M.D.
P.O. Box 2157
Champaign, IL 61820

Parent Music Resource Center
Tipper Gore
1500 Arlington Blvd.
Arlington, VA 22209
(703) 527-9466

To schedule Phil Phillips for interviews and speaking engagements, write to:

Child Affects
P.O. Box 68
Rockwall, TX 75087
Or call: (214) 771-9839 FAX (214) 722-1721

Appendix B

Signs and Symbols of the Occult

The following is an abbreviated list of common signs and symbols used in Satan worship and other occult practices.

Pentagram: This five-pointed star is used mostly in white magic by witches. It represents the basic elements of the earth (wind, fire, water, land) surrounded by the spirit world.

Hexagram: Although the world at large tends to think of this as a Star of David or the Crest of Solomon, noted Jewish symbols, the symbol was actually used by the Egyptians long before the Israelites adopted it as a symbol during their Babylonian captivity. Occultists consider the symbol to have considerable magical power.

Cross of Nero: This was known as the peace symbol during the 1960s. It is used today by heavy metal fans and occultists to symbolize a broken down-cast cross, and it represents the defeat of Christianity.

Ankh: This is an Egyptian symbol of life, especially fertility, and it is used in the occult as a symbol of the life or power given by Satan. Every major deity in ancient Egypt is depicted carrying this symbol. (Also known as the Ansata cross.)

Inverted Cross: The upside-down cross is often called the Southern Cross and it is used as a symbol to mock Christianity. It is a common tattoo for satanists. It is also used frequently as part of occult graffiti, and it has been made into a wide variety of jewelry items.

Swastika: This ancient religious symbol was used by occultists long before Hitler's time. It is known in ancient civilizations as the sun wheel and it supposedly represents the sun's course in the heavens to sun worshipers. Counterclockwise in the motion it depicts, the symbol also depicts movement away from the godhead.

Udjat: The all-seeing eye. Very often an eye shape is used by itself and placed in a third eye position to signify the same thing. A common symbol in Buddhist literature.

Scarab: The dung beetle is the ancient symbol of reincarnation (Egyptian). It is also a symbol of Beelzebub, the Lord of the Flies, which is the name used for Satan in the New Testament of the Bible.

Lightning Bolts: A jagged lightning bolt sign is referred to as a "satanic S" in occult practices. It is a symbol for the power of Satan when combined with other symbols.

Black Mass Symbols: Both symbols are used to indicate a Black Mass, which is a satanic service that parodies the Catholic Mass. During a Black Mass, the Lord's Prayer is often recited backward, holy items are usually defiled in some way, and unbaptized infants are symbolically sacrificed (and in some cases, actually sacrificed).

666: This number represents the Great Beast or the Antichrist in the book of Revelation in the Bible. The number six throughout the Bible is a symbol for man (the day of creation in the book of Genesis in which man was made). The use of three "6" figures creates a trinity—in this case a "human trinity" and the number has come to represent the "human godhead" or the supreme Antichrist, humanistic power.

Appendix C

Glossary of Occult Terms

A

Acolytes: Initiates; those in training to assume higher powers.

Altar: A table used to hold artifacts during rituals. It may be made of wood, stone, or earth. In some forms of satanic worship, a nude woman is used as the altar.

Amulet: A charm or an ornament worn to ward off evil spells, disease, or calamity.

Ancient One(s): The officiating priestess at a Black Mass is sometimes called the Ancient One (regardless of age); the term refers to those who wish ill for mankind.

Animism: Worship of the spirit presumed to inhabit all things (especially inanimate objects, plants, and animals).

Antichrist: Enemy of Christ. Any spirit or person opposed to Jesus Christ; also refers to the supreme world ruler anticipated in the book of Revelation as Christ's number-one enemy.

Arcana: A secret formula or process, especially part of Tarot cards. (Twenty-two pictorial cards make up the Major-Arcana, and fifty-six—or fifty-two—cards are divided into four suits as the Minor Arcana.)

Astral Projection: The process of a person's spirit traveling outside the natural body, sometimes to great distances and on different planes of consciousness.

Astrology: The practice of telling the future and answering life's basic questions by studying the position of the stars, moon, and sun.

Aura: The energy field that presumably surrounds all living things.

Automatic Writing: Writing done while the person is in a trance. The pen is supposedly directed by spiritual forces and the words written are often supernatural or prophetic messages, sometimes written in a language unknown to the person holding the pen. The penmanship is also often dissimilar to the normal handwriting of the person holding the pen.

B

Baal: Chief god of the Canaanites. Also Baal-Berith (Canaanite, "Lord of the Covenant"), Baal-Peor (Moabite, "Lord of the opening," a god of uncleanness).

Baalzebub: Hebrew name for "Lord of the Flies" (also spelled Beelzebub). One of the most powerful demons, also used as another name for Satan. Regarded as the demon of decay.

Basilisk: Legendary lizard, dragon, serpent. His breath or look was considered fatal.

Bells: They are usually rung to begin and end rituals.

Beltane: A Celtic spring festival celebrated on May Day and considered one of the major witches' sabbaths.

Black: Color most often associated with Satan.

Black Mass: Parody of Catholic Mass. The central act is usually the desecration of a host container (host being the bread representing the body of Christ) that has been stolen from a church. The host is "consecrated" by a satanic priest by defecating or urinating on the vessel containing it.

Blood: The drinking of human blood is considered a means of acquiring the divine qualities and the power of the person from whom the blood has been taken.

C

Caldron: Container in which magical concoctions are brewed or stirred.

Candles: Used in all rituals and ceremonies. Black candles are common. The combination of black and red candles signifies death or some form of black rite and incantation, including sacrifice.

Celebrant: The presiding priest at a ceremony.

Chalice: Goblet for blood, wine, water. Considered a symbol for woman in rituals.

Charm: An incantation or object believed to have special powers.

Child Sacrifice: Worship of Moloch first noted for this (in writings of Old Testament). Child sacrifice appears in various books on the occult as a part of a Black Mass.

Christian Spiritualist Church: An organization that promotes mediums and spiritists and is anything but Christian in doctrine.

Church of Satan: Headed by occultist Anton LaVey, this organization promoted the development of animal instincts, free sexuality, and self-indulgence. Members often held Black Masses. The group reportedly disbanded in 1975 and has been replaced by the Temple of Set.

Church of the Satanic Brotherhood: Founded in 1972 by former members of the Church of Satan.

Circle: A real or an imaginary circle is usually drawn nine feet in diameter on a floor during a ritual as a focal point for calling demonic spirits and powers. Magic is done inside the circle for protection and concentration.

Clairvoyance: Images form in the mind's eye as to past, present, or future events in the physical world.

Colors: Nearly always symbolic in their ritualistic, occult use—black: evil, Satan, devils; blue: pornography, water; green: nature, cleansing, soothing; red: blood, sex, energy; white: purity, innocence; yellow: power, wealth, perfection; purple: power, ambition.

Conjuring: Summoning a demon.

Coven: Group of witches who gather together for ceremonies. Common number of members in a coven is thirteen.

Crystal Ball: Determining the future by gazing into a glass ball or other object.

Curse: A spell or charm invoked against someone or something.

D

Dagon: Babylonian god.

Demon: A nonhuman spirit. According to the Bible, demons are angels who, along with Lucifer, rebelled against God and fell to the earth; they seek to embody living creations of God to spread their rebellion.

Demonology: The study of demons and evil spirits, including all of the manmade rites and ceremonies associated with them.

Devil: Refers usually to Satan or Lucifer; may also be a synonym for *demon.*

Divination: Attempting to gain information about people or events by studying natural phenomena to discern supernatural meaning.

Dragon: Frequently used symbol for Satan; Revelation 20:2 in the Bible refers to Satan as "the dragon."

Druids: Celtic priests in ancient Britain and Gaul who were skilled in astronomy and medicine. They worshiped the sun and believed in reincarnation.

Dungeons & Dragons: A game in which demonology, witchcraft, voodoo, blasphemy, insanity, sex perversion, satanic rituals, sadism, necromancy, divination, various forms of killing (assassination, suicide, cannibalism), and desecration are included in fantasy role-playing.

E

Evil Eye: Superstition credits certain people with the ability to cause harm through their gaze; wearing charms or amulets supposedly makes a person immune from the effects of an evil eye.

Exorcism: Delivering a person from demonic control. Occultists also use the word to refer to purifying something from nonoccult influences.

F

Familiar Spirit: A demonic spirit that does the bidding of a witch or medium; may also be an animal indwelled by a demonic spirit. Often just called a familiar—a demonic spirit that acts as an intimate servant providing supernatural counseling and aid.

Fire: Symbol frequently used for Satan.

Full Moon: Attributed to have great magical power; prime time for occult rituals.

G

Ghost: The spirit of a dead person according to occultists. Christians consider ghosts to be demons masquerading as the dead.

Goat: Satan is believed to appear frequently in the form of a goat; the goat's head has been a symbol for Satan since the sixteenth century.

Grimoire: A book of spells; generally the property of a witch or a coven.

H

Halloween: October 31, considered the day of the year most suitable for magic or demonic activity; believed by occultists to be the time when the souls of the dead revisit their former homes; a major witches' holiday.

Hecate: Goddess of the Lower Regions and the patroness of witchcraft.

Horned God: Part man, part goat; symbol of male sexuality in witchcraft.

Horoscope: Chart showing a person's destiny as determined by astrological studies.

I

I Ching: Chinese book of divination at least three thousand years old; the book most associated with Confucius and other taoists. In occult practices, it is used to gauge the flow of yin and yang energies and to determine actions a person should take to balance positive and negative forces. Usually fifty harrow sticks—long and short—are divided into heaps, and the pattern of short and long sticks is read according to the *I Ching* manual. Coins may also be used.

Incantations: Using repeated words, phrases, or sounds to produce magical effects.

K

Karma: The belief that a person's position in this life is the result of bad or good things done in a previous life.

Key of Solomon: The most famous book of spells; legends claim it was written by demons and hidden under King Solomon's throne. It has been translated into various versions used today in occult practices.

L

Levitation: The act of raising a person or an object from the ground and causing it to float through the air by supernatural power.

Lucifer: One of three archangels in heaven, cast from heaven for leading a revolt of angels against the power of God; another name for Satan.

Luciferans: A medieval satanic sect in the thirteenth century that made sacrifices to demons, worshiped Lucifer, and considered Satan a "brother" who was wrongfully treated by God.

Lycanthropy: When an occultist takes on an animal form, such as a werewolf. Includes a belief that people can change themselves into plants or animals.

M

Magic: Attempting to influence or control people or events by supernatural means. Black magic is done with an evil intent, calling devils, demons, and evil spirits to cause harm to another person. White magic is intended for healing or positive purposes. Magical ceremonies regularly feature rituals, symbols, costumes, dramatic invocations to spirits, and incense.

Magic Circle: When a circle is drawn on a floor and used for magical ceremonies; the magical powers are believed to protect those in the circle from evil.

Martial Arts: Rooted in the concept of weaponless fighting, these skills combine mental, physical, and spiritual energies into various modes of self-defense, or the achievement of paranormal feats of strength and control. Their systematic use causes them to become a mystical religion to many participants.

Master: The chief or leader.

Materialization: The physical manifestation of a spirit being.

Medium: One who acts as an intermediary between the world of spirits and normal reality. Spirits are often summoned during a seance, through Ouija board communications, through a series of rappings and knocks, or through automatic writing, painting, or drawing. The medium, from a Christian perspective, openly invites the indwelling presence of demons to take control of one's body or environment.

Mental Telepathy: Using mental images to receive and transmit messages.

Mentor: Senior brothers and sisters.

N

Necromancy: Communicating with the supposed spirits of the dead, usually by holding a bone or some other part of a corpse.

Numerology: Divination by using numbers associated with a person's name and birthdate.

O

Occult: That which is beyond the realm of human comprehension; literally means a "secret beyond rational understanding." Used to describe a wide range of activities related to man's attempt to understand and manipulate the supernatural for his own purposes.

Omen: A prophetic sign.

Ouija Board: A board with numbers and letters through which spirits supposedly can communicate by guiding a template across the board.

Owl: The bird most commonly associated with evil powers, death, and misfortune.

P

Pagan: One who is not a Christian, Jew, or Moslem; a heathen. The new pagans are an organized group that seek to revive a religion based on the worship of nature and the lunar goddess.

Palmistry: Interpreting the lines and form of the palm of the hand.
Parapsychology: The study of occult phenomena, such as precognition, clairvoyance, and mental telepathy.
Poltergeist: Considered to be a noisy ghost—generally one that throws objects, breaks objects, causes mischief; may also be a term applied to a person with tendencies to be a medium.
Power Object: An object believed to have transferred witch power to cast a spell when placed in the presence of an unsuspecting person.
Precognition: The ability to see into the future.
Premonition: A foreboding sense about events in the future.
Prophecy: Ability to foretell the future.
Psychic: Pertaining to phenomena that are supernatural or demonic; a person who has such power.
Psychometry: Attempting to gain impressions from a physical object owned or worn by another person to tell about the owner's history or whereabouts.

R

Right-Hand Path: Considered the esoteric path toward spiritual illumination and positive goals to mystics and occultists. It is also called the path of light. The left-hand path is associated with darkness, evil, bestiality, and black magic.
Ritual: Any activity or tool intended to focus the power of individuals toward a group concern or object.
Runes: Occult symbols found in many areas of North Europe, used for magic; from the German word *raunen,* which means "secret" or "mystery."

S

Sabbat: The seasonal assembly of witches in honor of the Archfiend.
Sacrifice: An offering made to a deity, usually on an altar. Occult sacrifices are performed ritually to placate a god and to offer blood, the foremost symbol of life. Many occultists believe that the ritual slaughter of a sacrificial animal releases life energy that can be tapped magically and used by the magician to enter the spirit realm.
Satan: The foremost enemy of God; called variously by these names, among others:

The Adversary
Apollyon (Destroyer)
Archfiend
Antichrist
Asmodeus
Astorath
Behemoth
Beelzebub (Lord of the Flies)
Demon
The Devil

Diabolus
Grand Master
Lucifer
Mephistopheles
Mulciber
Old Horned One
Set (Egyptian)

Satanic: Pertaining to Satan or evil.
Satanism: The worship of Satan as supreme god.
Seance: Ritual in which a medium supposedly summons the spirits of the dead.
Serpent: Serpents with horns are symbolic of demons.
Shaman: A medicine man or witch.
Silver: The metal of preference in occult jewelry and for occult objects.
Soothsayer: A medium.
Sorcerer: A wizard, witch, or magician who practices black magic.
Sorcery: Magic, usually black magic. The use of magical paraphernalia to harness supernatural powers, including the use of occult formulas, mystic mutterings, and incantations.
Spell: An incantation designed to produce magical results.
Spirit Guide: A demon impersonating a person (often long deceased) to give advice upon request; also known as a familiar.
Spirits: Often considered to be the spirits of ancestors or those who are dead, believed to influence the world of the living; includes demonic spirits, which are fallen angels.
Spiritism: The worship of or communication with supposed spirits of the dead.

T

Talisman: An object believed to have magical powers.
Tarot Cards: A series of cards used for divination.
Telekinesis: Moving objects through the air or across a room by occult power.
Telepathy: Mind-to-mind communication by mental images, not words or signs.
Theosophy: Literally means "wisdom of God"; a religion that has some Christian concepts but also includes reincarnation, karma, and spiritistic practices.
Transcendental Meditation: A religious system noted for its use of a mantra (personal secret words) to release inner powers and to invoke relaxation, energy, and a sense of well-being. The use of mantras comes directly from the Hindu yoga tradition.
Triangle, Trinity: A symbol that in occult circles invites a spirit to appear; magicians study triangles and the number three.

U

Uroboros: A symbol showing a serpent eating its tail; used to express unity between a sacrificer and his sacrifice.

V

Vampire: According to legends, one who rises from the grave by night to consume the blood of persons.

Voodoo: The use of spells, sorcery, potions, and fetishes to control the actions of another person.

W

Warlock: Male witch.

Werewolf: According to legend, a person who has the ability to turn himself (or who has been turned) into a wolflike creature.

White Magic: Magic that is supposedly helpful or beneficial; most serious occultists do not make the distinction between white and black magic, and neither does the Bible.

Witch: One who practices magic.

Witchcraft: The practice of sorcery or magic.

Witches' Sabbath: Meeting of a witches' coven; a time for the performance of magical rites and ceremonies. Usually includes gathering around a bonfire or caldron, lighting black candles, and performing various rituals and sacrifices. Often culminates in a sexual orgy.

Wizard: Male witch.

Wraith: A projected astral body.

Z

Zodiac: The pattern of stars and planets used in astrology.